Velma Fischer

Velma Fischer

Crafts for Fun and Profit

WOMAN ALIVE

Crafts for Fun and Profit

by Eleanor Van Zandt

Aldus Books London

Series Coordinator: John Mason

Design Director: Guenther Radtke

Picture Editor: Peter Cook

Designer: Ann Dunn

Research: Ann Fisher
        Marian Pullen

Copy Editor: Damian Grint

Projects Consultant: Walter Fischman

Series Consultants: Beppie Harrison
               Jo Sandilands

About This Book

This is a crafts book with a difference. Here at last is a no-nonsense, easy-to-follow guide to a wide range of craft skills, especially prepared for the busy housewife with absolutely no previous experience and the minimum of special equipment. To make sure of this, we set a team of beginners to work, and they made most of the objects pictured in these pages. You can, too. The book starts from scratch with every project — there are 18 of them — and explains every technique with simple instructions and clear step-by-step color photographs. We have used diagrams only where photos simply don't show the technique clearly enough. The book is arranged so that you learn each technique by first making one attractive and useful object — a colorful rug for the living room floor, a splendid set of eye-catching party candles, a handsome mosaic coffee table. Other photographs show more ambitious items that you can go on to make, using variations of the same basic technique. A final section includes a whole range of Christmas projects for you and your family to make. A question-and-answer section on marketing your wares and a list of books for the reader who wants to perfect her skills complete the book.

Contents

The Need to Create

We all enjoy making something with our hands. Finding the right medium for one's own special talents is very satisfying— whether it's yarn and knitting needles, a lump of clay, or oil paint, brush, and canvas.

Below: the sheer joy of creating something —without worrying about standards of excellence—is a feeling most of us experience before we grow up and become self-conscious.

Above: spinning, weaving, and embroidery were the usual creative outlets for women— rich as well as poor—when this picture was painted 400 years ago by an Italian artist.

Right: although machine-knits are available today, many women—like this Victorian lady—enjoy knitting garments by hand.

Left: the pleasure of handling the materials is a major element in the enjoyment of crafts.

Above: for some people, creative expression is not just a pastime, but a serious pursuit—as it is for the British sculptor Elizabeth Frink, seen here at work in her studio.

Crafts for Everyday

Originally, people learned crafts in order to provide necessities for their homes. The idea of making these objects beautiful, as well as useful, followed naturally.

Above: pottery is one of the oldest crafts. Vessels for eating, drinking, and cooking were needed early in man's development.

Right: the need for something warm underfoot stimulated the craft of rug-weaving.

Above: in hot climates, the nicest thing underfoot is cool stone. The Romans used stones to make mosaic floors of great beauty.

Left: drafty castles could be made a little cozier with tapestries, which, by the 1400's, had become very elaborate. This French tapestry depicts a lady with her spinning.

Right: no longer needed as a source of light, candles are still valued for their distinctive shapes and colors and for their warm glow.

Crafts to Live By

Today, most of the articles we use are made by machine, with mass production methods. But in earlier times, making things by hand was not only a source of satisfaction but a source of income as well.

Above: this 17th-century Dutch painting evokes a time when lacemaking by hand was a major industry. Today, it is still practiced by a few nimble-fingered old ladies.

Left: having opted out of the "rat-race," many hippies manage to gain a small income by making and selling objects such as bead necklaces or the soft toys shown here.

Below: this young woman at work on a modern pottery figure is fortunate in having a steady job, and a creative one, working for the Gustavsberg ceramic factory in Sweden.

Left: this Spanish girl brings a few extra pesetas to the family with her embroidery.

Below left: spinning and weaving of wool is still an at-home industry in parts of Scotland.

Below: tourism brings a demand for hand-made objects, such as Madeira wickerwork.

Crafts as Art

Today, many artists are turning to crafts as means of expression. In their hands materials take new and unusual forms, showing the great scope offered by the craft fields.

Right: the Persian rug woven by these women may someday hang in a museum, as many do today—regarded as works of art.

Below: a spectacular use of mosaic, by the Mexican artist Juan O'Gorman, adorns this university building in Mexico City.

Left: ancient Peruvian pottery may have partly inspired this boldly patterned jug by Picasso, but it bears the stamp of the artist's unique imagination.

Below left: "La Prima Donna" is an assemblage of found materials, including an old radio cabinet, and bicycle handlebars, put together by artist Jacqueline Fogel.

Below: actress Julie Christie wears a sweater designed by Elizabeth Frink, who sculpted the bronze "bird" as well. The sweater, one of a limited number, sells for about $100. A special frame is available for displaying it.

The Crafts Revival

Today, people are discovering the pleasure of creating. Leisure hours become productive hours, and the making and owning of hand made objects brings special satisfaction in our mass-produced world.

Below: the quilting bee, which enlivened long winter evenings on the frontier, is once again a popular activity.

Above: encouraging children to develop their talents is another satisfying dimension in craft work. Here, a mother and son enjoy painting faces on eggshells.

Above left: self-expression is a way to self-understanding for many patients in mental hospitals. These people paint to express their fears and to relieve tension.

Left: summer in a large city brings outdoor art and craft exhibits. Here, a view of New York's Lower Manhattan is part of the show.

Above: an ancient craft from North Africa, now very popular, macramé—or creative knotting—can be used for fashionable garments, like this pretty and easy-to-make vest.

A Mosaic Table
1

If your creative instincts freeze in the presence of modeling clay and go positively numb at the sight of brush and canvas, you'll be delighted by the simplicity and sheer fun of mosaic tile. It's so easy—simpler, even, than painting by numbers. And because you can change your design as many times as you like by moving the tiles around before fixing them, you can be relaxed about the whole thing. Yet with a little practice you'll be able to turn out beautiful articles that people can use and enjoy.

The coffee table shown here, for example, was designed and made by a beginner in only a few days. She decided on a symmetrical design with an Indian flavor, and you may want to begin your mosaic work with a variation of this pattern. But use imagination and your own choice of colors.

Ideas for mosaic designs are all around you. A sketch clipped from a magazine, a pattern copied from some fabric you especially like, even your child's happy scribblings, could inspire a colorful mosaic.

To make a coffee table similar to ours, you will need:

Opaque glass mosaic tiles. These can be purchased in hobby shops, hardware stores, and department stores. We used a total of about 7 pounds, or $4\frac{1}{2}$ square feet, of tiles to cover an area 24 by 30 inches.

Tile nippers. With these you can cut tiles into irregular shapes, useful for filling in small gaps in the design.

Impact adhesive. This is used to fasten the tiles to the surface and to apply plastic stripping to the edge of the table. Apply this with a squeeze bottle or with a glue spreader.

Below: a proud hostess and capable craftswoman entertains on her first mosaic-tile project, a handsome coffee-table.

Right: before beginning work, she assembles the materials she will need to make the table: wood base and table legs, plastic mixing bowl, rag, grout powder, sponge, palette knife, adhesive, nippers, and an assortment of tiles. Optional: plastic stripping for a neat edge, and silicone "sealer" to protect the finish.

Grout. This is a cement used to fill in the cracks between the tiles. It can be bought as a ready-mixed powder.

A piece of plywood, or other wood, at least $\frac{3}{4}$ of an inch thick, to serve as the base for the mosaic. If the board has not been coated against moisture, you should give it two coats of varnish and allow these to dry thoroughly before beginning your mosaic.

Plastic stripping (optional) to give the table a neat edge. This should be about 1 inch wide and cut into four lengths equaling the four sides of the table. It can be purchased in do-it-yourself shops.

Four screw-on table legs from a do-it-yourself shop, a hardware store, or a lumber yard.

Silicone "sealer" (optional), from most hobby shops, for protecting the finished mosaic.

Also needed (and probably already in your kitchen): a *plastic mixing bowl,* the kind used for dishwashing or hand laundry; a *rag*; a *sponge*; a *putty* or *palette knife,* and some *rubber gloves* to protect your hands.

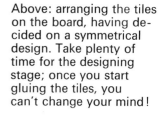

Above: arranging the tiles on the board, having decided on a symmetrical design. Take plenty of time for the designing stage; once you start gluing the tiles, you can't change your mind!

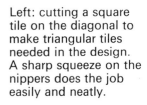

Left: cutting a square tile on the diagonal to make triangular tiles needed in the design. A sharp squeeze on the nippers does the job easily and neatly.

Right: applying adhesive to the back of a tile. Notice the loose tile, lifted off the board to make it easier to position the glued tile.

Technique

1. Design is first. Move the tiles around on the board until you get a design that you find pleasing. Shift, change, scrap the whole idea and start over from scratch if necessary. Leave a space between tiles, as this will be needed later for the grout filling.

2. Where you need smaller tiles in the design, use the nippers to cut them. You'll soon master the knack of using these. Because the individual tiles are so cheap, you'll never notice the waste from your learning sessions. For a diagonal cut, hold the nippers and tile as shown in the picture opposite. For tiny squares, cut parallel to the edge. To remove corners or create irregular shapes, use a cutting technique known as "nibbling." In a series of squeezes on the handle of the nippers, nibble off bits of tile until you obtain the size and shape

you need. Don't worry if the cut edge is a little off-target; mosaic is not an exact art.

3. Once you have finished your design, you can begin to glue the tiles to the board. This is very easy. You simply leave the tiles in place on the board, then glue one at a time to the board with adhesive. Each time you lift a tile for gluing, remove an adjacent tile as well. This will give you a little space in which to maneuver. Don't worry about excess adhesive oozing slightly around the tiles as they are tucked into place. The grout will cover this. But do be careful to leave space around each tile for the grout.

4. Allow the glue to dry thoroughly. This will take about 24 hours.

5. If you want to give your table an attractive smooth edge, attach plastic strips with adhesive to the edge, making sure that the top edge of the plastic is flush with the top of the tiles.

6. Grout the surface of the table. Into your mixing bowl pour about 3-4 cupfuls of the

Above: working the grout into the spaces between the tiles. Pieces of plastic stripping, applied to the edge of the table beforehand, make a neat finish. Below: a damp sponge and plenty of elbow grease remove excess grout from the surface of the tiles. Tiny particles can later be removed from the tiles with the help of a moistened nail brush.

Right: legs are screwed into the base, and the table is ready for use. If you wish, you can then apply a coat of silicone "sealer" to protect tiles and grout.

grout powder. Add water and work the mixture with a palette knife or with your fingers to form a paste about the consistency of cake frosting. The proper texture is important. If the grout is too thin, cracks will appear when it has dried; if too thick, it will be difficult to spread between the tiles. Be sure, also, that no lumps remain in the mixture. When the mixture is ready, dump it onto the surface of the table. Using a rag, spread it around, pushing it into the crevices between the tiles. You'll get no extra points for neatness here. It's thoroughness that counts.

7. Clean excess grout off the surface of the tiles, using a sponge or rag moistened with cold water. Don't attempt a complete clean-up job at this stage, as you don't want to remove any of the grout filling. The idea is simply to remove most of the excess while it is still moist, and so save yourself some work later on. At this point, it's a good idea to wash out the mixing bowl, so as to prevent the remaining grout from drying in it and spoiling the bowl.

8. Leave the table top to dry overnight.

9. Next day, inspect the surface to see if the spaces between the tiles are well-filled with grout. If you find bubbles or cracks, mix a little more grout and apply where necessary. Clean the surface again. When the grout has dried thoroughly, complete the clean-up job. Make sure that the top surface of each tile, including corners, is exposed. Some grout will probably have collected in the tiny pits on the surface of each tile. A nail brush will help you remove these particles. The beauty of your mosaic depends on each tile being clean and glistening, so don't skimp on the cleaning.

10. Attach the screw-on legs to the underside of the table.

11. Cover the surface with a damp cloth or plastic sheet and leave it covered for three or four days. Keeping the cement slightly moist for a few days makes it set more solidly later.

12. If desired, apply a coat of silicone "sealer" to protect the table from stains.

Left: these three vases were made with opaque glass tiles set directly into the grout. Stylized fish decorate the two smaller vases, and the large vase has a geometrical abstract design.

Right: a dramatic frame for a mirror, made of glass mosaic tiles.

Far right: these flower pot containers, like the vases at left, were made by setting tiles into grout, over a foundation of cardboard and wire mesh. A hole was left in the bottom of each pot for drainage.

More Mosaic

After your first venture into mosaic work, you'll want to branch out into new kinds of projects. Mosaics can beautify many different objects, as you can see from the photographs on these pages. Ash trays, cigarette boxes, jewel boxes, and lamps are some of the other possibilities. You could also add a charming touch to your kitchen with a canister set, made from coffee cans decorated with mosaic matching the kitchen curtains or wallpaper. Or make a mosaic shelf to put on top of an unsightly radiator. Or give a dull bathroom a feeling of Roman opulence with a wall mosaic.

Of course these various kinds of mosaic require varied techniques. Some involve setting the tiles or stones directly into cement; some involve making a design beforehand and transferring it to the surface to be decorated. Your craft shop should be able to supply you with instructions and materials for these projects.

One exciting aspect of mosaic work is the great range of textures you can use. Your hobby shop will probably stock ceramic tiles as well as glass ones. But that's only the beginning. Comb the beach for colorful, smooth pebbles. Try bits of stained glass, or shards of broken crockery. Once you become proficient, you may decide the time has come to work with marble and semi-precious stones.

From simple designs, you can move into more ambitious subjects. A photo of your pet cat or dog could be adapted for mosaic treatment. A mosaic version of a favorite painting is another exciting possibility.

Such elaborate mosaics demand not only skill in handling the materials, but also a good understanding of shading, perspective, and the different effects produced by various shapes, colors, and sizes of mosaic stones. Keep your eyes open and try to find mosaics to study. You'll find them decorating many modern buildings.

Below: this plate and flower container were made with the simplest of all mosaic techniques: the application of ceramic tiles that come in sheets on a mesh backing. A simple design can be created by removing some tiles from the sheet and inserting others in a contrasting color.

Below: this beautiful wall-mosaic of an old German city was made with a combination of marble, red sandstone, and green, brown, red, and ocher ceramic tiles. The sharp details of the design are softened slightly by the subtle blending of different shades of each color within each area.

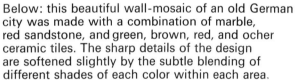

Bead Necklaces

2

How many times have you searched for exactly the right necklace to wear with a certain dress, blouse, or sweater? You find the right colors but the wrong style, or the right style and colors but a big price tag.

Why not solve the problem with your own hands? You can string sophisticated necklaces in a great range of styles to complement everything in your wardrobe.

The basic one-strand rope of beads is, of course, easiest. Then you can move on to all sorts of variations: knotted beads, "suspended" beads, multi-strand necklaces, and even elaborate collars like the beautiful ones shown on page 31. Some wire and pliers will expand your range as you can see in the photos on pages 32-35.

The materials you'll need, to make both strung and wire necklaces, include:

Beads. A good notions department or shop can supply you with a variety. Junk shops offer not only old necklaces with usable beads but also beaded handbags and garments. And don't forget the out-of-fashion costume jewelry in your dresser drawer. Salvage the beads for a new necklace.

Thread. Strong nylon thread, including some "invisible" thread, is most useful.

Clasps. These can be purchased in craft shops.

Scissors and a *needle*.

Wire. You can use copper, silver, or silver-plated wire. A medium-fine gauge produces best results.

Wire cutters. Available in hardware stores.

Pliers. You will need both flat-nosed and round-nosed pliers, also obtainable in hardware stores. Be sure to buy pliers with smooth inside jaws.

Emery paper (also called wet-and-dry paper) should be purchased in a medium-fine grade.

Left: deciding which necklace to wear can be a pleasant problem when you have a large number to choose from. Make them yourself for a few pennies each, and wait for the compliments.

Right: all the materials you'll need to make glamorous necklaces for yourself and your friends. Start making a collection of beads— the variety of sizes, shapes, and colors will give you plenty of ideas.

Below: nothing could be easier than stringing beads—even children do it! And if you use stiff thread, you can even dispense with the needle.

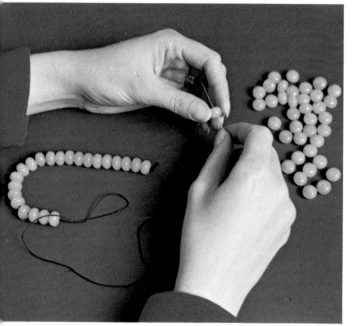

Stringing the Beads

Plain ropes of beads present no problems. Just thread the needle and string away. If the necklace is long enough, you don't even need a clasp.

But this is only the beginning of bead necklaces. Look on the next page to see what you can aspire to once you've learned a few basic stringing techniques. First, practice the techniques by making the simple necklaces shown here. The diagrams show what you do with the thread to create each of the different effects.

When making a necklace requiring a clasp, first tie one end of the thread around a pencil or other small object, leaving a few inches for attaching the clasp later. Use good long lengths of thread in making these necklaces. For the one shown at right, you will need a double thickness.

28

Left: string beads until necklace is 2 or 3 inches long. String four more beads, and then draw the thread again through the first of these four beads and pull it taut, forming a loop, as shown in the diagram. String three more beads, then repeat the loop pattern as many times as desired. Alternating large and small beads, as in the photograph, will help to conceal the thread.

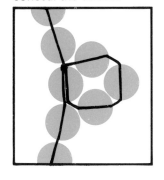

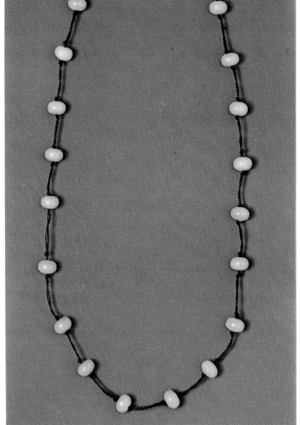

Left: the beads are spaced about 1½ inches apart by making a knot on each side of a bead, as shown in this diagram. Tie the knot as close to the bead as possible. Slip a needle into the knot and slide it along until it is next to the bead. To get even spaces between the beads, cut a strip of card to the required length, and use this card as a gauge.

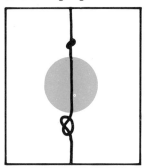

Left: a double thread, divided as shown in the diagram, is used for this necklace. String 5 or 6 inches of oblong beads. Next, alternate round and oblong, ending with a round bead. Divide the thread. String 13 each of round and oblong beads on one strand, plus a few inches of small beads. Then secure the end. Thread the other length of nylon through both large and small beads to make a shorter length. Then thread it through the already-strung beads until you reach the end. Attach the clasp.

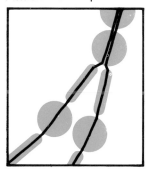

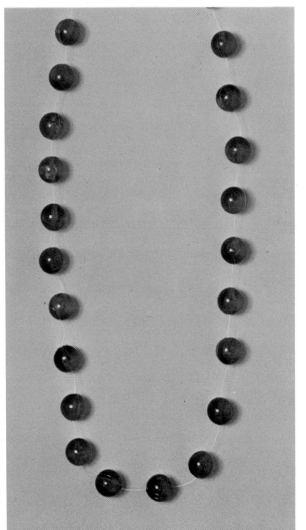

Left: a "suspended" effect can be created with monofilament, transparent nylon. String the thread through the bead, then bring it around over the bead and through the hole again. Knot the threads at the bottom of the bead and pull the knot taut, as shown in the diagram. Monofilament thread is very strong and is good for use with transparent beads. The pictures on the following pages give you an idea of the beautiful necklaces you can create, using these basic techniques.

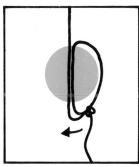

Left: a necklace with an African flavor, made of leather and large beads—very effective with a low-cut dress.

Right: especially suitable for brunettes or redheads, this necklace has the glamour of a theatrical first night. Not for beginners, but something to aim for later.

More Strung Necklaces

Once you've practiced the basic techniques described and illustrated, you may want to try more complicated designs.

Elaborate collars like those shown here call for lots of patience and careful planning before you begin to string. After you've chosen your beads, spread them out on a towel and play around with them until you get an effect you like. Then draw a diagram showing which beads would go where. You needn't draw the whole necklace—just a section of it, showing the pattern. But plan the size carefully. Use any single strand of beads to help you decide how the finished necklace should lie on your neck. Use this length as a guide in planning your necklace. Make another diagram, showing how the threads will run through the beads (like the

diagrams shown on page 29, but larger, as necessary). If your necklace is very complicated, use different-colored pencils to indicate the various threads.

In planning your necklace, remember that you will get a more supple strand if you intersperse the larger beads with small beads or with knots. This will also produce a more interesting line.

You can make very striking necklaces using fine leather thongs in place of thread. Use large beads and knot the leather on each side of the bead. Or run the leather through three small beads in a row, pull them into a cluster and tie the leather in a single knot. Continue making clusters at regular intervals. (Of course, you can use leather and beads to make belts as well.)

Finally, why not try making your own beads? Hardware and craft shops offer plastic material that can be formed into beads, polished, and painted.

Left: a choker and some long necklaces made with tiny beads and shells. The one at left uses the wire link technique described on the following pages.

Right: equal parts of romance and elegance make this necklace. It would be perfect with a long white gown.

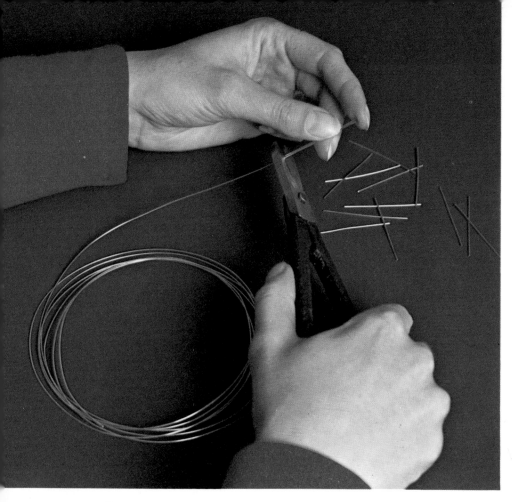

Left: cutting lengths of wire. The wire should be straightened out with the fingers before cutting.

Below: making loops using round-nosed pliers. The loop must be pulled slightly downward so that it is centered along the wire's axis.

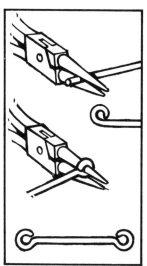

Wiring the Beads

An ordinary necklace of blue beads, bought at a chain store, was transformed into a handsome accessory (shown on page 34) by carefully spacing the beads out with links of silver wire.

You can make a similar necklace easily and quickly. The procedure is not so complicated as it seems at first glance, and you can work many variations on the basic technique. (See pages 34-35.)

For a necklace of the length shown in the picture you will need 32 beads. (You may use more or fewer, but an even number in any case.) They should all be the same size; graduated beads are not appropriate for this style, although they are fine for others.

1. Straighten the wire between your fingers. (This is one reason why you should go for the rather fine wire, as thicker wire can't be handled so easily.)

2. Cut 16 lengths of wire, each $1\frac{1}{2}$ inches long. These will be the lengths between the beads. If your beads are rather large, you'll want to increase the length of each piece of wire. Conversely, if the beads are quite small you can reduce the length and perhaps add more links. Use your own taste to get good proportion.

3. Rub the ends of the wires on the emery paper to smooth away sharp edges and burrs. (Sharp edges will catch on clothing and scratch the skin.) It is important that the smoothing be done at this stage—it can't be done after the wire is bent. Run the wire over the back of your hand to check for any roughness.

4. Using the round-nosed pliers, grasp one end of one of the wires (see diagram) and bend it back toward the main part of the wire

Right: threading two beads on a piece of wire and making a loose loop at each end.

Below: the diagram shows the same process. The loops are not quite complete, so that they can be hooked into the other, finished loops.

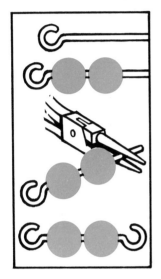

until it touches the wire. Next, grasp the loop with the pliers so that one of the round jaws is under the joint, and bend the loop downward until the axis of the wire is centered on the loop (see diagram). Make similar loops at each end of all the wires.

5. Tighten the loops with the flat-nosed pliers. Then check each loop to make sure that it is flat when looked at along the *length* of the wire. If a loop appears slightly crooked, correct this with the flat-nosed pliers. Put the finished wires to one side.

6. Cut 16 more lengths of wire, which will hold the beads. To find the correct length for these wires, first cut one piece of wire, say, 2 inches long. Loop one end as you have done before, thread two beads onto the wire, and judge how much wire will be needed for another loop. Cut off the excess wire, and make the remaining loop. If this length is correct, unloop both ends, remove the beads, and straighten out the wire. Measure it, and cut 16 pieces of this length.

Discard the trial wire, as it will probably not bend back again very well after being bent the first time.

7. Rub the ends of wire with emery paper as before to make them smooth.

8. Now you are ready to thread the beads and assemble the necklace. Loop one end of a wire, but not too tightly, using the round-nosed pliers. Thread two beads onto this wire, and make another loose loop at the other end. Now hook one loop through a finished loop on one of the wire links. Tighten the loop, using the flat-nosed pliers. Attach the other loop to another link in the same way. Continue assembling the necklace, alternating two beads on a wire with one link, until it is finished. Check all the loops and tighten them where necessary. You may find that the necklace has a twist. If this happens, cut out one link and replace it with another, rotating one of its loops 90°. This should eliminate the twist.

Your necklace is now ready to wear.

Right: linking a wire-with-beads to a plain wire. Take special care to close all loops firmly and evenly.

Below: this diagram shows the linking process in more detail.

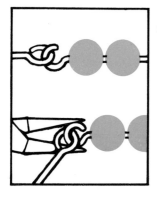

Below: the completed necklace. You now have a distinctive piece of jewelry, easily made.

You can, of course, work many variations on this link technique. For example, put single beads on pieces of wire and alternate these with wire covered with baguettes (tubular beads). The only wire to be seen on the finished necklace will be the loops.

On the other hand, if you want to feature the wire, you can work pieces of it around a knitting needle, twisting it first one way and then the other, to make a scroll-like design. Alternate the curved wire with beads.

The wire-and-bead technique is useful for making bracelets and earrings, as well as necklaces. Clip-on findings (metal bases for jewelry) and wires for pierced ears are available at craft shops. Drop-shaped beads look good as earrings, and as necklaces too. Try alternating them with round beads.

A distinctive look can be achieved using single loops of wire (about $\frac{1}{4}$ of an inch in diameter), hammered to make them flat. This makes them slightly irregular. You can make an entire necklace or bracelet with such loops (varying the sizes), or use them in combination with beads.

More Necklaces with Wire

For a dramatic, fashionable piece of jewelry, make a wire collar necklace. These use the same techniques that you learned for the blue bead necklace, but have a completely different look. They are especially effective with low-cut dresses and with high-necked sweaters.

First place a length of silver wire around your neck and note the length required. Allow another one and a half inches and cut the wire at that point. Using round-nosed pliers, make a large loop at one end and a large hook at the other. This forms the catch. Pendant beads and loops are attached with small loops. Study the necklaces pictured here and you'll understand the technique.

Reminiscent of American Indian jewelry, this pretty necklace is well-suited to a sweater or to any simple dress with either a high or a low neckline.

Collar-type necklaces are especially flattering worn with low-cut dresses, as these two pictures illustrate. Simplicity is the keynote here.

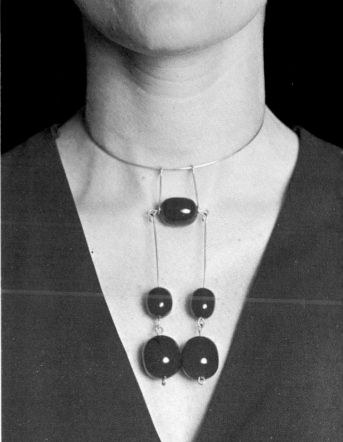

Bottle Art
3

Before you throw those empty bottles away, or take them back to the store for the deposit, have another look at them. You'll probably find a few among them that have pretty or unusual shapes. With a bit of imagination and some paint you can transform these bottles into strikingly beautiful and useful objects. The same goes for jars and glasses. A brightly painted jam jar can hold your kitchen spoons or knives. Apothecary jars can be used to hold any number of things; painted with your own designs they can become smart accessories, especially for the bathroom. And, of course, a selection of jars and bottles can be painted in a variety of colors to make lovely vases.

Once you acquire a little expertise in this easy craft, you can make charming gifts for your friends and relatives. A thoughtful gift for a family would be a set of tumblers painted with each member's zodiac sign. You can make an attractive desk set for your husband by painting a matching motif on a variety of containers: a medium-sized jar to hold pens and pencils; squat jars to hold paper clips, stamps, and rubber bands; and a large bottle—such as a Chianti bottle—to be used as a lamp base.

The materials you'll need for bottle-painting are few and inexpensive.
Bottles and jars are yours for the looking. Keep your eyes open for unusual shapes.
Paint. Special lacquers designed for painting on glass are most useful. You can also use poster paints or acrylic paints, provided that you cover the painted surface with a coat of clear lacquer. The paints can be mixed to obtain an unlimited number of shades. Experiment with small amounts.
Brushes. You should have several of these, in different sizes, including one about $\frac{1}{2}$ an inch wide for backgrounds, and some smaller ones for detail work. A sable brush is recommended for intricate patterns.
A soft pencil, for drawing designs.
Masking tape, useful in certain designs.
Paper, for making stencils.
Turpentine, or turpentine substitute, for cleaning the brushes.
Foil pie tins, or other containers, for paints.

Right: with a little paint and imagination you can transform ordinary bottles into beautiful objects like these—well worth displaying on a special shelf. They make welcome hostess gifts, as well.

Left: well-scrubbed, these bottles are ready for painting. The special lacquers for painting on glass can be mixed to obtain subtle colors. A roll of cellophane tape (not shown) is also useful.

Technique

1. Wash the bottle thoroughly with soapy water or detergent to remove grease and dirt. Careful cleaning is essential to ensure that the paint adheres properly. Dry the bottle with a clean cloth.

2. Working on a table covered with newspaper, apply the undercoat to the bottle with a fairly wide soft brush. Use long, even strokes, and work rather quickly—especially if the paint is one of the quick-drying varieties—in order to prevent an uneven surface. You can, of course, leave the bottle a solid color, particularly if it has an interesting shape. A very pleasing effect can be obtained on bottles made of thick glass by applying the undercoat to the inside of the bottle. Pour a little paint into the bottle and turn it around until the entire inner surface is covered. Then when you paint the design on the outside, you will produce an attractive three-dimensional effect.

3. To get a good solid background for your design you may want to apply a second undercoat. Allow the first coat to dry overnight, before applying the second. Then let the bottle dry for another day or two.

Note: Always clean your brushes immedi-

Above left: applying the undercoat to the bottle. A second coat may be needed with solid colors.

Above: a random pattern of flowers can be easily created by daubing on paint with the tip of a small brush, using a variety of colors.

Below: the finished bottle makes a charming. container for these dried flowers and grasses

ately after use. First swish them around in a small amount of turpentine or turpentine substitute, and then wash them under the tap with soap and water.

4. Apply the design to the bottle. As you can see from the picture on page 37, lots of different designs are possible.

The flower-splashed design on this page is one of the easiest. Load a small sable brush with plenty of paint and daub it onto the bottle in a little circle of dots. Put a different-colored dot in the center of the petals. Don't try to outline the petals or the center—the brush itself will do this.

One important thing to remember is that if you are using more than one color in your design you must allow one color to dry before putting another one next to it.

If you want to try a more ambitious design, such as the large stylized flowers on the left top and bottom bottles on page 37, you may prefer to sketch the design lightly on the bottle before painting it, using a chinagraph pencil (available in artists' supply stores).

Geometric designs, such as stripes or zigzags, are not nearly so difficult as they look. A bit of cellophane tape or masking tape will help you do the job and produce neat edges. Apply two rows of tape to the bottle, leaving a space between them that will be painted. Cut away any parts of the tape that cross this area, using a single-edge razor blade or sharp knife. Be careful not to chip the undercoat in the process. Make sure that the edges of the tape are tightly stuck to the bottle, so that paint cannot seep underneath. Paint the exposed area, going over the edges of the tape. Let the bottle dry for 24 hours before pulling the tape off.

5. If you have used poster or acrylic paint, give the finished bottle a coat of clear lacquer.
6. When the paint has dried, put the bottle into a cold oven, and bring the temperature to about halfway between 250° and 275°F. (130°C). Leave the oven at that temperature for about four or five minutes and then turn it off. Allow the bottle to cool down in the oven. The paint will then have a hard finish, resistant to heat and moisture.

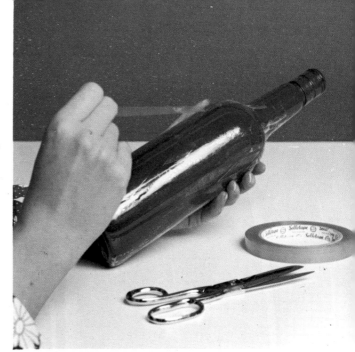

Above: applying cellophane tape in long, straight parallel strips before painting a zigzag pattern.

Below right: removing excess tape at the corners.

Below: painting the stripe.

Left: the finished bottle.

Left: rug-making is a craft the family can enjoy together—although the actual hooking requires a bit of strength in the hand. This little girl hands her mother the pre-cut pieces of yarn as they are needed.

Rug Hooking

4

It's easy to see why rug-making has remained one of the most popular of all crafts. For one thing, the product is so useful. A colorful rug not only provides warmth and comfort underfoot but also gives a bright accent to a room. Some rugs can be used as wall hangings. And you can use rug-hooking techniques to make chair-seat covers and cushions. Although it takes a bit of time and patience, hooking a rug is a very simple activity. Both short-tufted and shaggy rugs can be made from one or two simple techniques that you can learn in a few minutes. You can work while watching television or chatting with family or friends.

The first step, of course, is to choose the colors and design. If you have artistic talent, you may want to create your own design, or adapt a motif from some curtain fabric or wall paper. To do this, you use a mesh backing that has every tenth thread marked with a color (such as the one shown in the photograph on page 42). Trace the design onto some thin paper. Decide on the size you want the finished design to be, and count the number of marked threads (on the mesh) that it will cover, measuring in one direction only. For example, suppose you are doing a single full-blown rose, and the diameter of the rose will go across six of the colored lines on the mesh. Now, with a pencil and ruler make six evenly spaced lines across your drawing. Let's say that the distance between these lines is $\frac{1}{2}$ an inch. Next, draw some lines crossing the first lines at right angles and space them $\frac{1}{2}$ an inch apart, also. Make as many lines as you need in order to cover the whole design with a grid pattern. This small grid pattern will

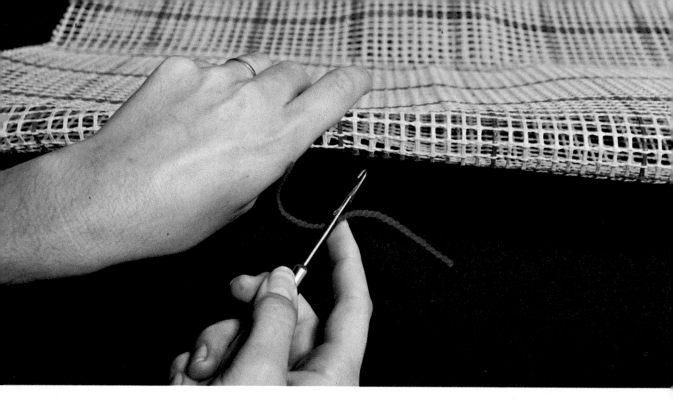

serve as a guide in sketching your design onto the large grid on the mesh backing.

Fortunately, you don't have to be an artist to make a beautiful rug. Various companies sell rug patterns in a great range of styles, and some offer ready-packed kits, containing all the materials you will need.

If you are assembling your own materials —for a short-tufted rug, such as the one in our picture—you will need to buy:

A latch hook (shown in the photo above).
Mesh backing. This can be purchased in needlework shops, either plain, or with a grid pattern, or a design on it.
Rug yarn. This comes in pre-cut packs as well as in skeins that you can cut yourself. For a short-tufted rug you will need about $7\frac{3}{4}$ pounds of yarn, or 46 cut packs (320 pieces each) per square yard.

If you cut your own yarn, you'll need:
A cutting gauge. This is an oblong piece of wood with a groove in one edge, which is also used in making rya rugs (see page 46). The distance around the gauge should be nearly 3 inches.

To finish the edge of the rug, you will also need some *extra yarn*, a large *needle, scissors,* and (if the rug is circular) some *carpet braid* about 2 inches wide.

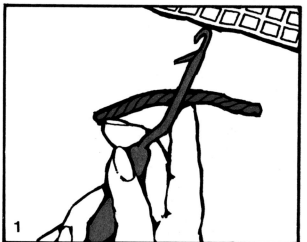

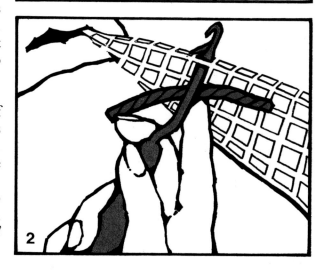

Left: the special mesh backing used in making a hooked rug and the correct position for holding the hook. The red lines help in planning your design.

Below: these diagrams and those on the following page illustrate the steps in hooking the Smyrna knot. In making short-tufted rugs, you use one strand at a time.

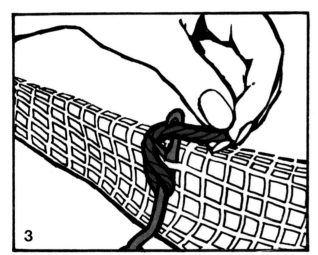

3

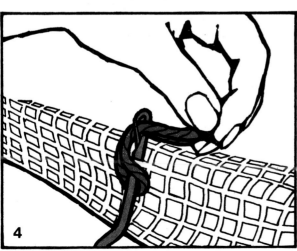

4

Technique

In hooking a rug, work one row at a time, changing colors as the pattern requires. Do not fill in parts of the pattern separately, as this will give an uneven pile. Work from left to right if you are right-handed, from right to left if you are left-handed. You will probably find it comfortable to work at a table, moving the worked portion of the rug into your lap as you progress. A weight placed on the unworked canvas will help to keep the rug stationary.

1. If you have bought your yarn in skeins, begin by cutting a number of pieces in each color. Wind the yarn evenly around the cutting gauge until it is covered with one thickness of yarn. Then cut along the groove with scissors or a razor blade.

2. Before starting to hook, hem one end of the canvas. (This applies to a rectangular rug; for a circular or oval rug, see below.) Fold one of the cut edges back about two inches, with the raw edge on top. Crease the fold sharply along one thread and make sure that threads are exactly superimposed lengthwise and crosswise. Tack the hem in place. The first few rows of your knotting will be through this double thickness of mesh.

3. Now you are ready to begin knotting. (This knot, incidentally, is called a Smyrna knot.)

Pick up a strand of yarn and hold it against the latch hook with your index finger as shown in Diagram 1.

Insert the hook in one hole and push it up through the next hole (Diagram 2) until the latch clears the mesh.

With your other hand grasp the two ends of the yarn and pull them taut and upward, around the hook, making sure that the ends are even. Then pull the ends sideways, around the latch and under the hook (Diagram 3).

Still holding the yarn ends, begin to pull the hook back toward you. As it slides

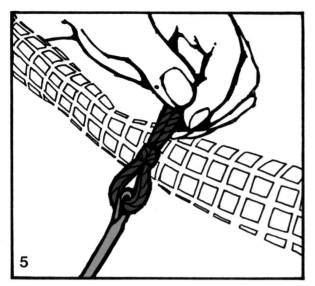

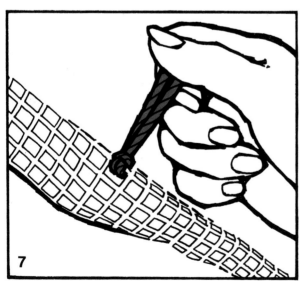

under the mesh, the latch will close Diagram 4).

Continue pulling until both ends have come through the loop and the hook slides off (Diagrams 5 and 6).

Pull the ends taut (as shown in Diagram 7). If one end is a bit shorter than the other, pull it up to make them even.

4. Continue in this way, knotting row by row, and changing color where necessary. When you get within a few inches of the end, turn up that edge to make a hem. Knot through this double thickness to the end.

(There is another way of making the Smyrna knot, which produces a knot that slants in the opposite direction. This method must be used, along with the first method, in order to make all the pile lie the same way, if two people are working on the rug at the same time. A rug-hooking kit will give instructions for this second technique.)

When you have finished knotting the rug, bind all four edges with yarn in a shade that matches or blends with the color at the edge of the rug. Hold the rug with the wrong side toward you. Using a large needle and a length of yarn, anchor the yarn by making several overcast stitches in one hole. Bring the yarn up through the hole toward you, then diagonally over the edge and up through the fourth hole. Then bring the yarn back in the opposite direction, over the edge, and up through the second hole. Then forward into the fifth hole, back into the third, and so on around all four edges. This will make a good sturdy binding.

To make a circular or oval rug, you proceed very much as for a rectangular rug. Starting at one edge (your first row will be only a few knots long), you continue knotting in straight rows from edge to edge.

To finish the edge of a circular or oval rug, trim the canvas around the worked areas, leaving a margin of about $1\frac{3}{4}$ inches. Turn this back over the wrong side of the rug and pin carpet braid to it. Stitch the braid to the canvas at the edge of the rug. Then sew the inner edge of the braid to the canvas, making darts where necessary.

The Rya Look

Warm, informal, and inviting—that's the rya rug, a Scandinavian contribution to modern home decor. Actually, rya has been around for a long time. A variation of the shaggy rya pile was used to line jackets in Scandinavia back in the Middle Ages. Today, designers are using it on all sorts of things— from wall hangings to evening gowns.

Rya can be knotted on a loom or sewn onto a piece of canvas. On the following pages, we show you how to make a rug by the sewing method. But you can also make a rya rug using the same basic techniques you learned for the short-tufted rug. In fact, you can even buy a rya kit containing patterned canvas, pre-cut yarn, and latchet hook.

There are a few differences in technique. The canvas is woven so that the rows of knots are separated, to give a layered appearance. Also, you use three long thin strands of yarn, instead of one short thick one. By mixing several colors in one knot, (as shown in the diagram) you can give your rug extra interest and color excitement.

Shaggy rya rugs are warm and inviting, and they're perfect with modern decor. You can make them with a hook on mesh backing, as shown in the diagram.

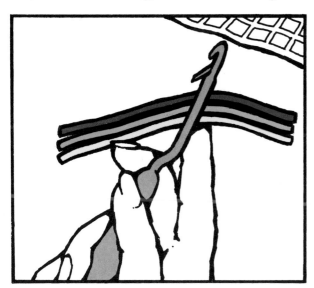

More Rya Rugs

The distinctive aspect of rya—whether used for a rug, a wall hanging, or an article of clothing—is its shaggy, irregular surface. The design in a rya rug changes subtly as the pile is moved this way and that. There are several ways to achieve this effect. The simple, hooking technique is shown on the previous page. Large rya rugs are generally made on a loom.

For a small rya rug or wall hanging, you might like to try the sewing technique. This method produces a slightly more irregular pile than is possible with the hook and the pre-cut lengths of yarn.

Materials you will need for the sewing method include:

Loosely woven cloth, such as needlepoint canvas. Some shops carry backing especially designed for rya work.

A needle with a very large eye.

Skeins of yarn. Standard rya yarn is somewhat thinner than most rug yarn. Any thin but strong yarn—including cotton, linen, and synthetics—can be used.

A gauge. This is a stick with a groove in it, around which you make the loops. If you cannot find a rya cutting gauge, use any smooth flat stick, about $1\frac{1}{2}$ to 2 inches wide. You can also use two or three fingers of your left hand—particularly if you are making a rug with a very long pile.

The diagrams on these pages show the rya knot used in the sewing method.

1. Draw your design on the backing. (You should have a duplicate design, showing the colors, handy for reference.)

2. Cut lengths of yarn, about $2\frac{1}{2}$ to 3 feet long. Thread the needle with two or more strands of yarn (you can mix colors).

3. Push the needle under a thread going from right to left. (Reverse these directions, if you are left-handed.)

4. Bring the yarn back to the right and sew through the next thread, as shown in Diagram 1. Pull to make the knot.

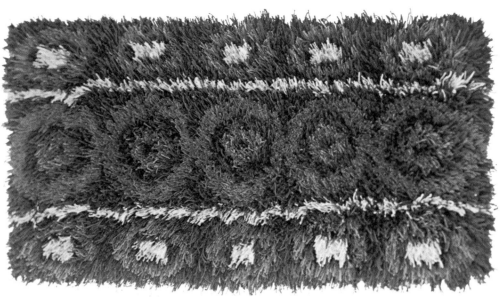

Above, left and right: small rya rugs like these can be made by the hooking or the sewing method—which tends to produce a slightly more irregular pile than the hook method. Some rya designs call for using two or more colors in the same knot.

Left: three strands may be used in the sewing method, but beginners may prefer to use only two strands of yarn. Three colors are used in the diagram in order to make the process clear.

Below, left and right: making a row of rya knots over a stick. For an even shaggier pile, you can use two or three fingers of your left hand instead of a stick, but this means having to cut the loops more often. A special backing fabric that has the rows marked is easiest to work on.

5. Now take the stick and lay it alongside the first knot, over the strands of yarn.
6. Bring the yarn up over the stick and make another knot, bringing the needle under the stick as shown in Diagram 2.
7. Continue making knots and looping the yarn over the stick.
8. Leave the stick in place, and cut the yarn along the groove or the edge of the stick, as shown in Diagram 3.
9. Continue sewing rows of knots—each successive row on top of the previous one. Change the color of your yarn as indicated by your design.

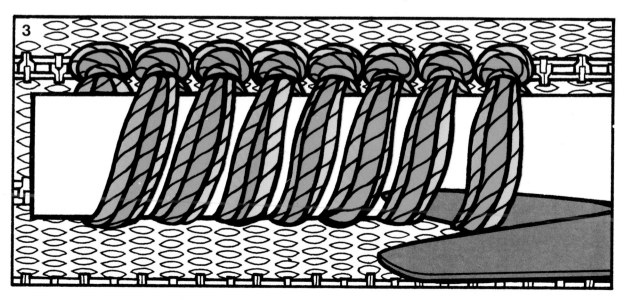

Candle Making
5

To our ancestors, there was probably nothing romantic about candlelight. It was simply all one had by way of light after the sun went down. Running out of candles meant sitting in the dark. And for a rural housewife, keeping a supply of candles on hand meant slaving away over a hot vat.

Today, electricity takes care of the lighting problem. We use candlelight instead to create a warm and festive atmosphere for a special occasion. And candle-making—far from being a chore—has become a popular hobby. You can make candles in a great array of shapes and colors. Surprisingly, some of the fanciest candles are among the easiest to make. The elegant candles on the opposite page, for example, are easily made with a purchased mold.

In your kitchen you already have some of the materials you need to make candles: a *burner*; two *saucepans*; a *pitcher*; a cake of *soap*; a kitchen *thermometer*.

From a candlemaker's supplier or craft shop you can get other basic materials:
Paraffin wax. This comes in powdered form or in blocks that can be broken with a hammer into manageable pieces.
Wax dyes, available as powder or solid.
Stearic acid (stearin). This is a flaky kind of wax in which the dye is dissolved.
Lengths of wick, in varying widths, are graded according to the width of candle they will burn efficiently.

To make a molded candle similar to ours, you will also need:
The mold. It's best to start with a shallow relief mold, such as the one illustrated.
Mold seal, or modeling clay.
A short stick, for holding the wick upright.
A mold stand. This holds the mold while the wax is being poured into it. You can also improvise a stand by placing two sticks across two level objects.
A bucket, deeper than the mold, and *two sticks*, longer than the bucket's diameter.

For a finishing touch, you will also need: water-soluble black *paint*; a *paintbrush*; and some *absorbent cotton*.

Right: you can give your parties an extra touch of glamour with elegant candles like these—and they're easy to make with a purchased mold.

Left: some of the materials you'll need for candles: paraffin wax, stearic acid, dyes, wicks, mold seal, a rubber mold, a mold stand, and a kitchen thermometer for testing the temperature of the wax.

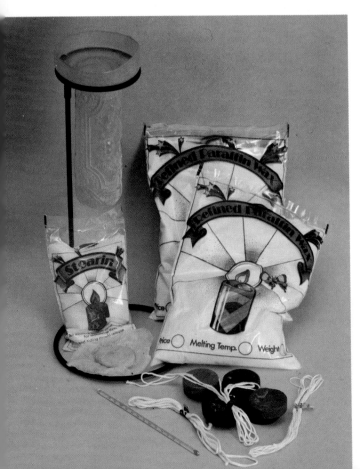

Technique

1. Select the correct wick for the candle you are making, and cut a piece approximately 4 inches longer than the length of the mold.
2. Have ready the bucket with sticks arranged as in the illustration at far right.
3. Measure the paraffin wax into one of the saucepans. For a 9-inch candle we used about 5 (U.S.) measuring cups ($2\frac{1}{2}$ pints) of powdered paraffin.
4. Measure the stearic acid into the other saucepan. Use 1 part stearic acid to 10 parts paraffin. For 5 cups of paraffin we used $\frac{1}{2}$ a cup of stearic acid.
5. Add the dye to the stearic acid. We used solid dye for our candle—$\frac{1}{4}$ of a tablet 2 inches in diameter and $\frac{1}{2}$ an inch thick. Flake the dye with a knife into the saucepan holding the stearic acid. Powdered dyes are very concentrated; a pinch of this dye will give plenty of color to 1 pint of wax. For an idea of the color of the finished candle, you can (after Step 8) dip a spoonful of the colored liquid wax into cold water. Solidified, it will be the color of the finished candle.
6. Slowly melt the paraffin over low heat. *Note*: great care must be taken in handling wax over heat. *Never* put it on high heat,

and never leave a saucepan unattended. Dip one end of the wick in the melted wax (to a depth of about 2 inches). Allow this to harden. The wax will keep moisture out of the wick during Step 13.
7. Make a very small hole in the top of the mold (using manicure scissors, a knitting needle, or some other sharp object) and thread the waxed wick through this hole so that there is about 1 inch of wick at the top of the mold. Apply mold seal or modeling clay around the hole at the top of the mold. Tie the other end of the wick around the short stick so that the stick will rest on the lip of the mold when it is inverted (see illustration on page 51). Place the mold on the mold stand or improvised rack.
8. Slowly melt the stearic acid-dye mixture. Do not allow it to overheat and smoke, as this will spoil the color. If the color isn't dark enough, you can now add more dye.
9. Add the melted stearic acid to the melted paraffin and reheat the mixture to 200°F (180°F, if it is a rubber mold). Test the temperature with a kitchen thermometer.
10. Pour the liquid wax into the suspended mold. You should have some wax left over for "topping up," as the wax will contract as it hardens, leaving a space in the top of the mold.
11. Tap the sides of the mold to release air

Far left: the dry ingredients, ready for melting. The pan at left holds paraffin: the pan at right, stearic acid and wax dye.

Left: testing the temperature of the liquid wax with a kitchen thermometer.

Below: pouring the liquid wax into the mold. The stick resting on the lip of the mold keeps the wick vertical.

bubbles. The bubbles will rise to the surface.
12. After about 3 or 4 minutes, transfer the mold to the bucket. If you use a mold stand such as ours, you can remove the ring with the mold, which helps to hold it steady.
13. Gradually pour cold water into the bucket. If wax starts to rise in the mold, stop pouring. You should be able to fill the bucket up to 1 inch from the top of the mold.
14. When a dip forms in the cooled wax, break the skin of the wax and top up the mold with some of the remaining liquid wax, after first reheating it to 180°F. This procedure may have to be repeated several times, until the bottom surface remains flat. Be careful not to overfill the mold, as this may cause wax to run down into the sides

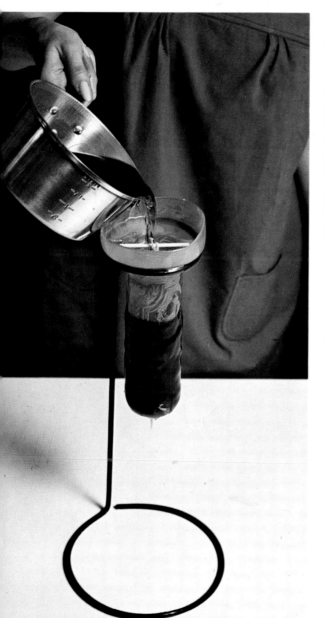

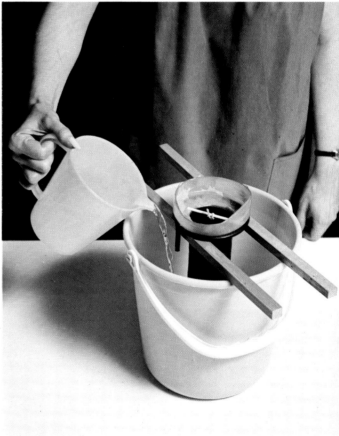

Above: with the mold (and removable ring) carefully balanced on sticks laid across the bucket, cold water is poured around the mold to assist in cooling the wax. Cooling takes about four hours.

of the mold, and spoil the shape of the candle.

15. When the candle is completely cold, after about 3 or 4 hours, lift it from the bucket and remove the mold. First pull the mold seal from the top. Then cover your hands with warm soapsuds and rub them over the mold. The moistened mold can then easily be peeled off the candle.

16. Remove the stick and the extra length of wick from the bottom of the candle. Scrape the bottom of the candle with a knife to make it level. Trim the wick at the top.

17. If you wish to highlight the relief on the candle, use a water-based paint. Mix the paint with a little water in a saucer. Using the brush, add a bit of lather from a bar of soap and mix well with the paint. (The soap helps the paint to cling to the candle.) Apply paint mainly to the recessed areas.

18. Go over the relief with slightly damp absorbent cotton, leaving some paint still remaining in the crevices.

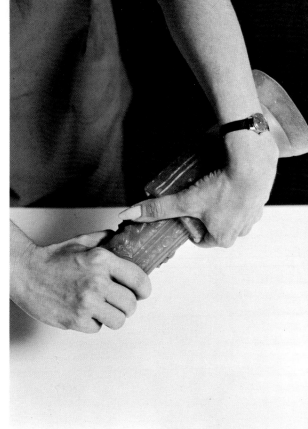

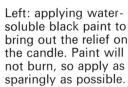

Above: having been moistened on the outside with warm soapy water, the mold is then peeled backward, releasing the hardened candle.

Left: applying water-soluble black paint to bring out the relief on the candle. Paint will not burn, so apply as sparingly as possible.

Left: wiping paint from the raised areas will produce a subtly highlighted effect.

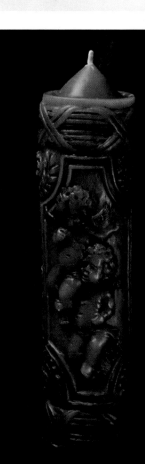

Right: the finished candle—a bit of baroque extravagance created easily and at small cost.

Hand-Shaped Candles

Hand-shaped candles can be made by either the dipping or the spooning method. The wax mixture is prepared in the same way as for the molded candles.

For dipping, you need a tall metal jug or pot filled with wax to a depth equal to the height of the finished candle. Tie the wick to a stick and immerse it repeatedly in the hot wax. Between each dip, allow the wax to harden for about half a minute. Re-heat the wax in the jug to keep it liquid.

If you do not have a very tall jug, you can make tapers by the spooning method:

1. Prepare paraffin, stearic acid, and dye, and gently heat the mixture.

2. Prepare the wick. Cut the wick to the desired length, plus enough to hold in the hand. Dip the wick into the saucepan and coat it with the liquid wax (except for the portion to be held). Allow it to dry in a straight line by pulling it taut and holding it in that position until it is stiff (about half a minute).

3. When the wax has reached 180°F, remove the pan from the heat.

4. Hold the wick over the pan, and spoon hot wax down it. Rotate the wick between the fingers for an even shape. Allow the surface to cool between each pouring. You may have to reheat the wax to bring it back to the required temperature.

5. After the candle has built up somewhat, allow it to cool slightly, then roll it over a sheet of clean paper. This will make the candle smooth and straight, and may be repeated several times between pourings.

6. When the candle has reached the desired size, coat it with wax heated to 200°F, and immediately immerse it in cold water to give it a glossy finish. Trim the wick.

Right: tapers can be made either by dipping the wick into wax or by the spoon method, shown here.

More Candles

Wax will do almost anything you want it to—as these pictures prove. After you've made a few candles, you'll want to experiment with various effects.

Sand-casting is one of the most ingenious techniques. You can use it to make unusual candles, such as the one shown at right. To make the mold, use a bucket or large box filled with sand and leveled at the top, but not packed tightly. Make a hollow in the sand using a dish or glass having the shape you want for your finished candle. The thickness of the sand coating will depend partly on how moist the sand is (moist sand produces a thinner shell) and partly on the temperature of the wax (hotter wax picks up more sand). A temperature of 212°F or higher is desirable—but never higher than 350°F. Remember to be very careful in handling wax at these higher temperatures. Pour the melted wax into the mold. As the wax is absorbed into the sand, you will have to top up the candle. When the candle has cooled slightly, make a

Above: a collection of colorful beeswax candles.

Above right: a tumbler was the mold for this candle. A small amount of clear wax was poured in, the glass rotated to coat the inside, and the excess wax discarded. Dye in several colors was swirled against the wax. Another coat of clear wax fixed the colors, and the mold was then filled with wax. A knitting needle helped in inserting the wick.

Below: a sand-cast candle gives out a warm glow.

Below: the spooning method described on page 53 was used to make this cheery red-and-white toadstool. Hand-shaping while the wax is warm can be used easily to create all sorts of interesting shapes.

Above: these candles were made with metal molds, tipped at angles to produce diagonal layers of wax. Each layer was allowed to set until almost hard before the next layer was poured into the mold.

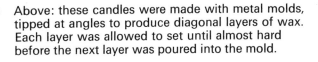

hole for the wick with a hot knitting needle. Stiffen the wick with wax, and insert it. When the candle is cool dig it out of the sand. Brush off the loose sand, and then smooth it with a knife to the desired shape.

Beeswax candles are strikingly different in texture and have a honey scent. Normally a warm soft yellow, sheets of beeswax are also available already dyed in various colors. They are easily rolled into cylinders and cones—although if the room is cold, you may need to warm the sheet gently. Work on a clean flat surface. Choose the correct wick for the size of the finished candle, and cut it a few inches longer than the sheet. Lay it along one edge, turn the edge over carefully to secure the wick, and roll the beeswax to the desired size. Press the edge against the candle to prevent it from unrolling. For a conical candle, cut the sheet into a right triangle. Begin rolling on the long side. Two triangles of different colors can be rolled together for an attractive effect, as shown in the photograph.

55

Setting in Clear Plastic

6

The 20th century might be called the Plastic Age. Plastics have transformed nearly everything we use. Not surprisingly, they play a part in many crafts described in this book.

Here is a craft in which plastic is not just a supporting player, but the star. Clear plastic is a beautiful, versatile substance that you can use to display all sorts of objects: coins, dried flowers, seashells, a favorite photo, an arrangement of old watch parts—just about anything. The sparkling clarity of the plastic makes the object appear suspended in space and gives it new interest from every angle. Using various kinds of molds, you can cast paperweights, keychain ornaments, bookends and the decorative parts of cuff links, brooches, and other pieces of jewelry.

Setting in clear plastic is a craft that can yield beautiful results. But—as in any activity involving chemistry—a certain amount of caution is required, not only to prevent accidents (liquid plastic is flammable), but also to get good results. Your first few efforts may be duds, so practice with objects that have no particular value, and leave great-granddad's watch for later.

In the following pages, we show you how to make an attractive paperweight. The materials you'll need for this project include:

Liquid plastic. Also called polyester resin, this is sold in cans and should be stored in a cool place. Buy the kind with the accelerator already added.

Hardener, or catalyst.

A measuring beaker, marked in millimeters, obtainable from a chemists' supplier.

A mold, suitable for a paperweight, made of polythene. (Molds made of various other substances, such as Pyrex glass and pottery—but *not* polystyrene—can be used instead.)

Dried flowers. Do not use flowers that have been dyed, as the dye will run.

Tweezers; and lollipop *sticks* for mixing.

Release agent wax (or any *non*-silicone wax) and a *soft cloth.*

Wet and dry sandpaper in three grades: rough, medium-fine, and very fine.

Metal polish, such as silver polish.

Cellophane or waxed paper, for your working surface.

Paper to cover the mold.

Rubber gloves or a barrier cream (optional) to protect your hands.

Left: a project the whole family can enjoy. With a little practice in working with clear plastic you can make beautiful objects like this paperweight. Right: materials needed in making a driedflower paperweight. Undyed flowers give best results.

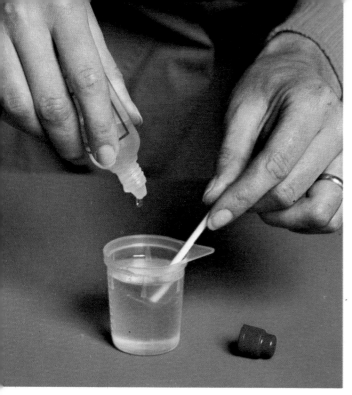

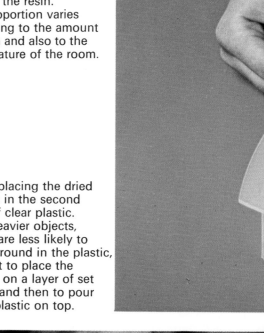

Left: adding the hard-
ener to the resin.
The proportion varies
according to the amount
of resin and also to the
temperature of the room.

Right: placing the dried
flowers in the second
layer of clear plastic.
With heavier objects,
which are less likely to
move around in the plastic,
it's best to place the
objects on a layer of set
plastic and then to pour
liquid plastic on top.

Technique

1. Wipe the inside of the mold with releasing wax and allow this to dry. Polish with a soft cloth. Repeat the waxing and polishing. Make sure that no excess wax is left in the corners. Do not touch the inside of the mold after the second polishing, as this will damage the protective surface. Cover the mold with a piece of paper to keep out dust.

2. Pour about 1 fl. oz. of resin into the beaker and add 9 drops of hardener. Using the stick, stir these together slowly.

3. Slowly pour the mixture into the mold. Allow this to set (covered) until it is tacky (usually about 4 hours).

4. Prepare another mixture of resin and hardener (the same amount as above) and pour this into the mold. Using the tweezers, place each of the dried flowers in the liquid plastic. While the plastic is still liquid, you can move the flowers around a little, using the tweezers. The flowers may shift by themselves, so check the mold after the first 15 minutes and reposition the flowers if necessary. It is also a good idea to check each layer every 15 minutes or so for the first hour

or two to make sure that no air bubbles have formed. If bubbles form, pierce with a pin.

5. Now mix $1\frac{2}{3}$ fl. oz. of resin and 15 drops of hardener. Pour this into the mold, and allow it to set until tacky. Continue, using this amount of resin and hardener each time, until the flowers are well covered.

The whole process of making the casting will take about four days, as you can only pour 2, or at most 3, layers in a day, and you will probably find that you need 7 to 9 layers in all. Note: never allow any layer to set solid for too long. This is because the plastic shrinks slightly as it hardens, moving away from the sides of the mold, so that a new layer of liquid plastic poured on top of the hard plastic might seep down the sides to the bottom. Don't be tempted to use larger quantities and make thicker layers. The hardening process generates heat, and thick layers of resin and hardener will react violently, causing the casting to split. Keep the layers $\frac{1}{4}$ of an inch deep.

6. When you have poured the last layer, leave the covered casting to set solid.

7. Remove the casting from the mold. First, turn the mold upside down and press on the base. Ease the sides of the mold away from the casting. The casting should begin to

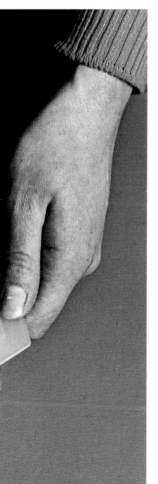

Left: pouring another layer of clear plastic over the flowers. Be sure to cover the mold with a sheet of paper between pourings, to prevent dust from settling on the plastic.

Right: removing the hardened casting from the mold. Immersing the mold in hot water may help in difficult cases, but this will give the mold a hazy surface, which means more work in sanding.

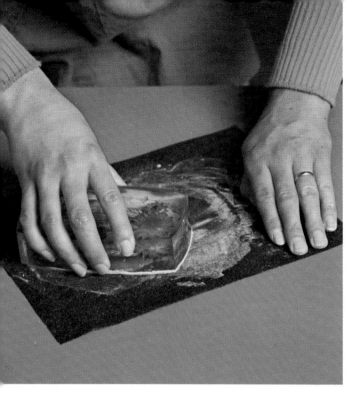

Above: sanding the casting with wet-and-dry paper and (right) polishing it with a rag and metal polish.

Right: beautiful and useful—the finished paperweight.

come away from the mold. If it does not, tap the lip of the mold against the edge of the table to release the casting. If you are using a Pyrex glass or pottery mold, which is inflexible, or if the polythene mold does not release the casting easily, you can immerse the mold completely in boiling water for 10 minutes, and then plunge it into cold water for another 10 minutes. If necessary, repeat this process. The castings will then drop out of the mold. Note: the drawback to this is that the plastic surface will become cloudy, meaning more sanding.

8. Using the rough grade wet-and-dry paper, rub both top and bottom surfaces of the paperweight to remove all imperfections. An easy way to do this is to lay the paper in the sink, rough side up, with the tap running slightly, and rub the casting over the paper using a vigorous circular motion.

9. Repeat this process, using, first, medium-fine paper, and then very fine paper, until the paperweight is quite smooth.

10. Using a soft cloth and metal polish, rub the surface until it is smooth and clear.

60

More Objects in Plastic

Until you acquire some expertise, it's best to confine your casting work to small objects —the size of the paperweight or smaller. Jewelry of clear plastic (see page 62) is easily and quickly made. The smaller amount of resin used for each layer will set faster than a large amount, and fewer layers are needed.

Many castings look best if they are given a colored backing. You can do this easily by dyeing the last layer of resin, using one of the special pigments available in craft shops. Add the dye *after* mixing the resin and hardener,

Below: clear plastic is a perfect way to display a ship model. The plastic protects the model from dust and damage and gives it a dramatic "flying" appearance, as if it's on a voyage through space.

Above: a beautiful mistake. Pouring too-thick layers caused this casting to split; but the play of light in the cracks gives the casting a sparkling effect and makes it well worth keeping.

Above: a coffee-table top with a Natural History motif. Molds were built up on the board base with strips of wood and were then treated with a synthetic primer. A thin layer of white resin was then poured into the molds to provide an attractive base.

Below left: a selection of castings made with round molds. Plastic makes a clever picture "frame" Right: an experienced craftsman made these fine desk ornaments. The square-cornered castings were faceted with the use of a lathe.

and mix it well to ensure even color. The next-to-last layer must be completely set; otherwise you will get an ugly blurred effect.

On larger castings you may want to place the objects in different planes, to produce an interesting "exploded" effect. This is easily done by adding them at different stages.

Setting in clear plastic is an ideal way to safeguard and display collections of coins, shells, rocks, and insects. Embed the name of each object beside it. Moths and butterflies present a problem, because their wings tend to lose color when they are embedded in plastic. You can prevent this by spraying the wings very lightly many times with a polyurethane varnish to seal the color. Fresh flowers must be treated with a special flower-preserving agent, available in craft shops.

Setting in clear plastic is an activity the whole family can work on together. Your children may find it useful for school projects. And they'll discover how taking pains over a task brings a sense of accomplishment.

Design Your Own T-Shirt
7

Mass-produced, ready-to-wear clothes have one problem: you're likely to see other people walking around in "your" clothes. In the case of most garments, there's not really much you can do about this except grin and bear it.

But now you can add your own personal touch to so many simple ready-made clothes by using special dyes that you paint onto the fabric. These are a mixture of cold dye and thickener, and they can be used on any fabric that takes cold dye—such as cotton, linen, or silk. This kind of dyeing allows you great control over the finished design. Unlike tie-dye and batik—explained in the following chapters—it gives you a "hard-edge" effect. If you want a crisp, clean design on your fabric, try this dye-painting. For a more random effect, try batik or—especially—tie-dye.

Start by painting this clever T-shirt for your child. The cost is small, and once you've gained some experience, you can go on to decorate various pieces of sportswear and other items.

Materials needed for this project include:
A cotton T-shirt.
Cold dye, dye thickener, and *dye fix.* Buy two shades of dye—dark brown and deep gold.
A measuring jug.
A piece of cardboard or a sheet of plastic.
A thick black pencil, or a pen and some India ink, for tracing the design onto paper.
A sheet of tracing paper.
A soft pencil to trace the design onto fabric.
A brush for painting on the dye. A No. 1 sable brush does nicely.
You'll also need some *detergent* and some straight *pins.*

Left: an ordinary T-shirt can be made into an appealing and individual garment for a child, with the use of dyes painted onto the fabric.

Below: tracing the drawing from a children's book using a black pencil. The sad mouth of the original drawing (visible through the paper) is changed to a happy one for the T-shirt.

Bottom: tracing the drawing onto the T-shirt. Be sure to smooth out the fabric, and pin it to the paper so as to keep it from slipping about.

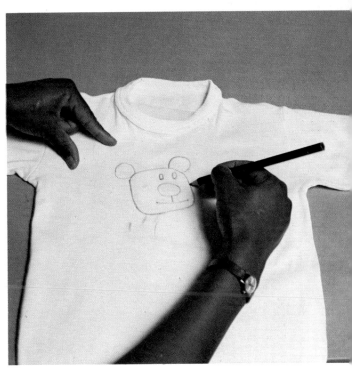

Technique

1. First wash the T-shirt to remove any fabric finish in it, let it dry, and iron it.
2. Trace the design onto the paper. Our instructions are for a drawing of a bear, which we took from a children's book. You can enlarge our drawing by sketching it freehand or by using finely ruled graph paper. Or find a similar drawing in a book of your own. Trace the design with black pencil or India ink so that it will show through the fabric.
3. Place the design under the shirt front and secure it with a few straight pins. Trace it onto the fabric using a soft pencil.
4. Place a sheet of cardboard or plastic under the material to prevent dye from seeping through to the other side.
5. Mix the dark brown dye according to the manufacturer's instructions.
6. Paint the outlines of the bear's body with the dye. Also paint the mouth, nose, and eyes. Allow the dye to dry thoroughly, away from direct heat. This will take anything from two to six hours.
7. Rinse the T-shirt well in cold water, then wash it in hot soapy water and rinse again. Allow it to dry and iron it.
8. Now mix the yellow dye, and paint in the bear's body. Carefully avoid painting over the dark brown lines. Allow the shirt to dry, then wash and rinse it as before.

Once the fabric has been thoroughly washed the colors are fast, and the garment can then be washed without fading.

You can, of course, paint on fabrics that are already dyed—you needn't restrict yourself to white. But remember that the resulting color will be a blend of the fabric color and the dye. That is, if you apply a blue dye to a yellow blouse, you will get green in the painted area—unless the blue is very dark and the yellow very pale. If you're in doubt about the effect, it's wise to cut a tiny piece of the fabric from the seam allowance and test the color.

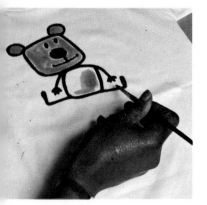

Above: painting the outlines of the bear's body with the dark brown dye-paint.

Left: filling in the body with the dark yellow paint.

Below: the finished T-shirt—color-fast and ready for all the rough wear a child can give it.

More Dye-painting

As you can see from the examples on these pages, dye-painting is a very versatile craft. Household linens lend themselves beautifully to this treatment. Put your initials on sheets and pillowcases. For a pattern, you can use large embroidery initial transfers. Iron them onto the fabric as you would for embroidery, and paint with the dye.

To get a really sharp edge on your designs, cut a stencil. Use a piece of fairly stiff paper or cardboard. Draw your design on the cardboard, then cut out the sections you want to be colored, using a cutting tool. Lay the stencil over the fabric (tape it around the edges to keep it from slipping), and paint over it with dye, using a rather wide brush. This is a good method to use if you want to make an all-over pattern on a piece of fabric before making it into a dress or a pair of curtains. The stencil will ensure that the motifs are regular and will give the printed fabric a professional look.

Right: a sophisticated use of dye-paint makes this long party dress a real show-stopper.

Below left: soft toys with personality are easy to create with a bit of imagination and some dye-paint. Effects formerly possible only with tedious appliqué are now quick and easy.

Below right: a striking "total look" for a dining area—bold swirls of color coordinate the tablecloth, the napkins, and the wall-hanging.

A Tie-dyed Scarf

8

Lovely surprises await you when you begin to tie-and-dye. This is a craft that offers real encouragement to the beginner. For example, the pretty scarf shown here is a "first attempt"! You, too, can achieve beautiful results with your very first project. And your children can join in. With a little practice they can even complete their own tie-dye projects, such as individual T-shirts in their own choice of colors and design.

Pleating and tying produced the pattern of the scarf shown here, but there are dozens of different techniques, each producing a different kind of effect. You can wrap the cloth in a nylon stocking, pinch it with clothes pins, tie objects up in it, and even pull it through plastic hair rollers! Even if you use the same technique and colors, you will get slightly different results every time. Each tie-dye project is unique. Removing the bindings to reveal a new, original design is always an exciting moment.

If you would like to make a scarf similar to the one pictured on the right you'll need: *White cotton fabric,* such as muslin, about 1 yard by 10 inches. Buy a yard or two, and you can cut this into strips and make several scarves.

Cold water dye, in two shades. Choose two colors that will blend well, such as pink and blue.

Dye fix. This is prepared by the manufacturer of the dye. Or you can use soda.

Thread for binding. This should be fairly strong, such as button thread. Other suitable materials for binding include yarn, string, tape, and rubber bands.

A plastic bowl. With cold water dye, you can also use bowls made of enamel ware, stainless steel, glass, or pottery.

A large measuring cup. Check the dye manufacturer's instructions regarding the amount of water to be added.

You'll also need: *scissors, rubber gloves, salt, washing powder,* a large *spoon,* and some *newspaper.*

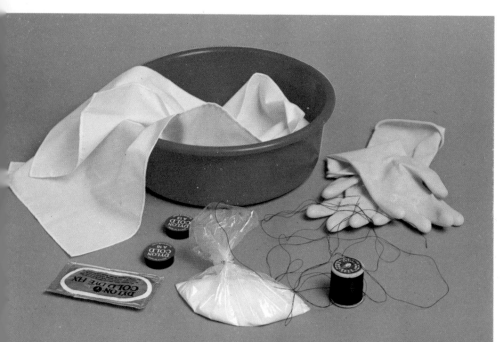

Right: this pretty scarf was made by a beginner! She simply pleated the fabric crosswise, bound it at intervals with some thread, and put it in some pink dye for an hour. Then she untied it, bound it up again, and re-dyed it in blue.

Left: materials you'll need for a tie-dyed scarf. Cold dye works well with all natural fibers, particularly cotton and linen.

Far left: pleating the material in regular folds. Ironing the cloth first helps make smooth pleats.

Left: binding the cloth. Make sure that areas you want to remain white are completely covered.

Below: immersing the bound fabric in the dye. The fabric should first be soaked in water to help keep the dye from the bound areas.

Technique

1. Begin by washing the fabric in hot water and soap, or detergent, to remove the finish. This will make the cloth more receptive to the dye. Press the cloth.

2. Pleat the cloth crosswise in accordion pleats about 1 inch deep.

3. Once folded, the cloth is ready for binding. The purpose of the binding is to prevent dye from reaching certain parts of the cloth. Where it is very tightly bunched together and covered by some material (in this case, thread), the cloth will not come in contact with the dye. Plan the pattern of your binding. You can make bands of varying thickness and at varying intervals, and you can also crisscross the thread between bands. Begin by placing your thumb near one end of the folded piece of cloth where you intend to bind. Place the thread under your thumb, leaving about 2 or 3 inches to lie loose along the length of the strip, covering the short end so that it will not slip. Remember that you must completely cover the material where you want it to remain undyed. Any bits of cotton showing through the binding will

70

receive the dye. To fasten off the thread, use a slip knot. Simply loop the thread very loosely once around the cloth, slip the thread through this loop, and pull it taut. This knot will hold fast during the dyeing. Move on to your other bindings. On a strip of fabric such as this, it is not necessary to fasten off and cut the thread after each area of binding. Simply make a slip knot, and move on to the next spot where you want to bind.

4. Prepare the dye. Wearing rubber gloves, prepare the lighter of the two shades of dye, following the manufacturer's instructions.

5. Before immersing your material, it is a good idea to soak it in cold water for a few moments. This is called "wetting out," and it helps to give a good "resist" to the dye—that is, it helps to keep the dye out of the bound areas. After soaking the cloth, squeeze it, or let it drain for a while, before putting it into the dye. If the dye does not completely cover the material, you can add some cold water, but keep this to the minimum.

6. Allow the fabric one hour in the dye, stirring it occasionally. Take it out of the dye and rinse it in cold water until the water is clear. When the water is clear, remove the bindings. This can be done while the material is wet. Find the end of the slip knot, and pull on this end. The thread will move beneath the loop securing it, enabling you to see it and pull it free. Then you can easily pull off all the binding in one motion.

7. After all the bindings have been removed, wash the fabric in hot soapy water and rinse until the water is clear. (Note: in washing tie-dyed garments, do not use products containing enzymes.) Dry and iron the cloth.

8. Now you are ready to add your second, darker color. Decide which areas you wish to leave white and which are to be left in the first color. Pleat the fabric as before, and bind these areas tightly. The areas left exposed will take the second color. Prepare the dye; wet out the bound fabric; and immerse it in the dye for one hour.

9. After rinsing, unbinding, washing, and ironing the fabric, hem it on all four sides—or fringe the ends. Your scarf is now ready.

Above: undoing the bindings after the first dyeing. The thread can be rewound on cardboard or an old spool and used over again.

Below: the cloth after the bindings have been removed. Now it must be washed in hot water to remove all excess dye. Cold-dyed fabrics can be washed often without fading.

More Tie-dyeing

A random look is part of the charm of tie-dye designs. One color blurs into another and no two parts of the design are exactly alike. Part of the fun lies in the surprise when you untie the fabric after dyeing.

Still you won't want your results to be a *complete* surprise, and you'll enjoy planning your effects by using different techniques. The pictures below show just a few.

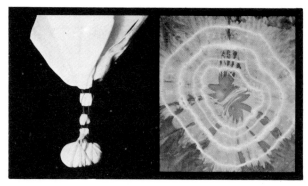

Above: tying knots in the fabric produces these "sunburst" patterns. Mark the positions of the knots with pencil or chalk before beginning to tie. Below: a series of knots produces a striped effect.

Above: the wavy concentric rings of this design are the result of tying a large stone in the fabric, crisscrossing it with thread, and binding the cloth at intervals to make the rings.

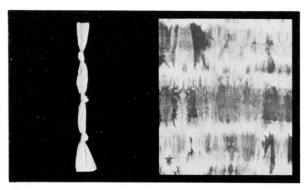

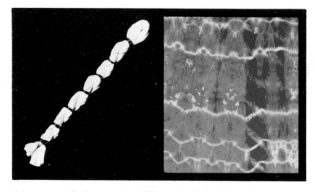

Below: a three-color, marbled effect can be made by crumpling the fabric into a tight ball and binding it with string in different directions. Re-form the ball and bind again for the second color.

Above: twisting and coiling the fabric back onto itself produces this interesting design. Below: This square-within-a-square was made by folding the fabric, stitching, and gathering.

First, you might vary the straight stripe on the scarf by diagonal pleating.

To make concentric circles, pull the cloth into points and bind around these points.

For a softly marbled effect, insert the fabric in an old nylon stocking and fasten the stocking at both ends with rubber bands. Place a few strong rubber bands around the filled stocking at irregular intervals.

Or squeeze the fabric tightly into a polythene bag. Fasten the bag at the neck and put a few rubber bands over the ball. Using a pin, poke tiny holes all over the plastic. The dye will seep through the holes into the cloth.

Binding objects into the cloth can produce some interesting results. Small stones are one possibility. Simply wrap the cloth around the stone and secure it with a rubber band. To make sure the resulting circles are where you want them, first mark the cloth with dots, using a pencil. For a pretty border print for a skirt, tie lots of small pebbles close together in a wide band near the edge of the fabric.

The possibilities of tie-and-dye aren't limited to clothing; you can also use it to add a lot of zing to your decor. A tie-dyed tablecloth in a radiating design, with napkins to match, can enliven your dining room. Or brighten up your bathroom with a tie-dyed shower curtain (use a plain plastic curtain as a liner). Look around your home for some corner that would be prettier and brighter with a bit of tie-and-dye.

Above: a child's T-shirt is made more individual with a tie-dyed pattern.

Right: A handsome waist-coat with a marbled look.

Above: coordinated colors and patterns in tie-dye decorate this living-room. The coffee table is covered with tie-dyed fabric under a sheet of glass.

Left: a "total look" in tie-dye gives this bedroom a special flair.

A Batik Wall Hanging

9

A touch of the exotic—made by you in your own kitchen—that's batik. This ancient craft probably originated in Java, and batik-dyed fabrics, such as our "sunshine face" wall hanging, do suggest the South Seas.

Basically, batik is a resist-dyeing process. That is, certain areas of a design are covered with wax to repel the dye. Then the wax is removed and these areas either left white or colored with another dye, with other areas blocked out.

A distinctive feature of batik is the "veins" running through the design. These are a result of the cracking of the dried wax, which allows a small amount of dye to seep into the blocked-out area.

Batik is a craft that takes a bit of practice, especially in the use of the *tjanting*—the "pen" used in applying the wax. You'll quickly acquire the knack of using it, but we suggest you practice with the tjanting on some scraps of material (see Step 7, page 77), before beginning the wall hanging. This design is a simple one, and with your preliminary practice, you'll find it very easy to make. For the wall hanging, you'll need the following materials:

Cotton fabric—a piece 20 by 20 inches.
Batik wax. This is a mixture of white paraffin and beeswax.
Cold water dyes that can be intermixed. This wall hanging uses red and yellow dye.
Urea, a dye-dissolver and color-brightener.
A liquid detergent, to remove excess dye.
Bicarbonate of soda, and *salt.*
A double boiler or saucepan (preferably enamel or aluminum) for melting the wax.
A candy thermometer.
A utensil for dyeing, a shallow pan.
A measuring jug, holding at least 1 pint.
A frame. This can be an old picture frame, or—ideally—a special batik frame.
A tjanting. This is available in craft shops.
Brushes, for applying wax to large areas.
A soft black pencil, for sketching the design.
Absorbent paper, such as newsprint.
Poster hangers; or two sticks of wood, 22 inches long, and some string.
Rubber gloves, thumb tacks, a sharp-pointed *knife,* a *teaspoon,* a *tablespoon,* and an *iron.*

Left: a simple design makes this wall hanging, done by a beginner. The cracks, or veins, are characteristic of batik designs.

Right: some of the materials and equipment you'll need to make a "sunshine face" wall hanging. In the center foreground is the tjanting, used in applying the hot wax.

Technique

1. Prepare the fabric. To remove its finish, immerse it in about 2 quarts of warm water, to which you have added 4 tablespoons of bicarbonate of soda. Rinse the fabric well, dry it, iron it, and hem it.

2. Before drawing the sun design on the fabric, sketch it on a sheet of paper the same size. Place a dinner plate upside down on the center of the square and draw around it. Sketch in the leaves around the sun. Practice drawing the face, as well.

3. When you've practiced making the design, you can draw it on the fabric. Lay the fabric down on a table. Place a few heavy books on the edge of the fabric to keep it smooth. (Or, if you're working on an old table that you don't mind scarring, pin the fabric down with tacks.) Using a soft pencil, draw only the outlines of the sun and the leaves—not the face or the veins of the leaves, which will be added later.

4. Stretch the fabric over the frame and tack it down so that it is taut. Arrange your work area so that the frame is very near the stove or hot plate on which you will heat the wax.

An electric hot plate is ideal for this purpose, as it can be placed on your work table.

5. Heat the wax in the double boiler or saucepan to a temperature of 200°F. Turn off the heat as soon as the wax has reached this temperature. *Boiling wax is dangerous and can burst into flames.* You may need to reheat the wax from time to time, to bring it back to the right temperature, but be careful! Don't get so absorbed in your work that you forget about the wax heating.

6. Using a large brush, block out the face of the sun with wax. As the wax goes onto the material, it should make the material transparent. This shows that you are using the wax at the correct temperature. Watch carefully, for if the wax is not hot enough, the dye may seep into this part of the fabric—which you want to remain white during the first dyeing.

7. Now outline the leaves using the tjanting.

Below left: tacking the fabric to the special batik frame. (An old picture frame can be used as an alternative.) Make sure that the material is taut, as this will make it easier to draw the design.

Below: applying the hot wax to the leaf outline, using the tjanting. The wax must be kept at a temperature of 200°F, which means checking it with a thermometer and reheating it occasionally.

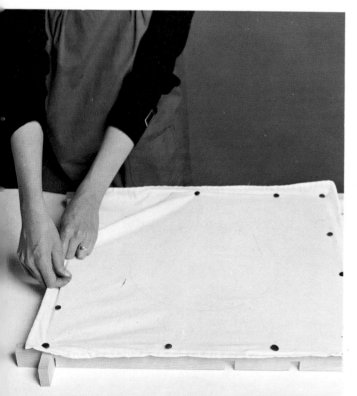

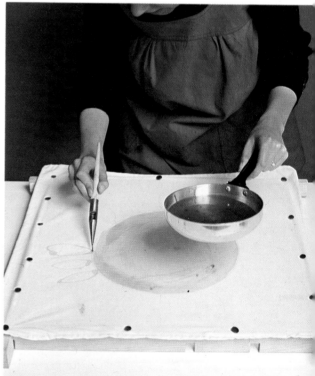

Above: immersing the fabric in the dye bath. The wax makes the fabric stiff. By crumpling it in your hands, you make cracks in the wax, causing the characteristic veins of dye to appear in the design.

Above right: ironing the wax out of the design. If the wax is rather thick, it's a good idea to scrape some of it off the fabric beforehand, then iron out the excess between the paper.

First, fold a rag and hold this in your left hand (or in your right, if you are left-handed). Dip the tjanting in the molten wax and fill the reservoir, not quite to the brim. Slip the rag under the tjanting so that no wax can drip out, and bring it over to the place where you are going to apply the wax. Move the tjanting along the line, holding it at a slight downward angle. Don't let it rest on the fabric, as this will impede the flow of the wax. Keep your two hands close together, so that when you want to stop drawing for any reason, you can immediately lay the tjanting on the rag. Drops of wax cannot easily be removed, although you can sometimes incorporate these into the design. Fill in the centers of the leaves with wax, using either the tjanting or a small brush.

8. Now draw the features of the face and the veins of the leaves by scraping lines onto the wax, using a sharp-pointed knife. Make sure the wax has hardened thoroughly before dyeing the fabric.

9. Prepare the red dye. Normally, it is preferable to begin with the lightest color and progress to the darker colors. In this particular case, however, we start with the red and then use the yellow, so that the background, which will be a blend of both colors, will be more of a pink-orange than a yellow-orange (which would have resulted from dyeing first yellow, then red). Follow the manufacturer's instructions in preparing the dye. Wearing your rubber gloves, put the fabric into the dye bath. By crushing the fabric slightly in your hands, you will obtain the characteristic cracks. Leave the fabric in the dye for the specified time, turning it occasionally.

10. Remove the fabric from the dye bath and allow it to drip over a sink. Hang it by one edge to prevent streaking.

11. When it has dried, iron out the wax. (If the wax is rather thick, you may want to scrape some off before beginning to iron.)

Place several thicknesses of blotting paper or newsprint on the table; lay the fabric, face up, over these; and place another sheet of paper on top. Using a fairly hot iron, go over the surface once. Remove the top sheet of paper, apply another in its place, and iron again. Continue ironing and changing the top sheet of paper until all the wax has been removed from the fabric.

12. Wash the fabric in very hot water containing some liquid detergent. Quite a lot of dye will come out, but plenty will remain in the fabric. Rinse until the water runs clear. Dry and iron the fabric and replace it on the frame.

13. Re-melt the wax. Apply wax to all the areas you want to remain pink—such as the facial features, the veins of the leaves, and perhaps the areas just around the leaves (which will make the leaves "stand out" nicely).

14. When the wax has hardened, re-dye the fabric in the yellow dye. Dry the fabric, iron out the wax, and rinse the fabric as before. Let it dry, and iron it.

15. To hang the wall hanging, attach it to poster hangers. Or make a hem in the top and bottom edges, run the sticks through these casings, and tie a length of string to each end of the upper stick.

Above: covering the areas that are to remain pink—such as the lines in the leaves—with wax.

Left: tidying up around the wax lines, using a sharp-pointed knife.

Below: immersing the fabric in the second, yellow, dye bath.

Below right: the finished wall hanging, ready to be attached to poster hangers and hung up.

More Batik

The possibilities of batik—in fashion as well as home decorating—are suggested in these few photos. A book explaining the finer points of the craft will show you lots more examples, and some beautiful designs.

In planning your batik projects, select your material carefully. Silk—particularly Japanese raw silk—is good for scarves and dresses, and it takes the dye beautifully. Fine cotton also works well in making garments. Cotton, or even linen, can be used for wall hangings, tablecloths, and lampshades, although linen is not so easy to work with. You may find it necessary to apply wax on both sides of the linen if it is fairly heavy fabric. Also, the distinctive cracks are somewhat more difficult to achieve. But if you are planning a rather bold design, it can look very effective on linen, which has an especially pleasing texture. Whatever fabric you choose, it must be white at the outset.

A dramatic effect can be achieved with the use of one colored dye plus black, leaving some areas white. Crush the waxed area well before the black dyeing, so that black veins spread throughout the design.

Above: this sophisticated batik scarf is made of cream-colored silk, dyed red and purple. The colors are muted by the original color of the scarf, and blended by a dense network of batik "veins."

Right: a simple dress made up in a batik-dyed fabric becomes an exotic eye-catcher.

Below: these colorful batik lampshades are made of lawn applied to iron-on stiffening.

A Colorful Lampshade
10

You may not be able to have breakfast at Tiffany's, but you can enjoy breakfast, lunch, and dinner under this eye-catching Tiffany-style lampshade. It's decorated with a brand-new kind of enamel that requires no heat and dries to a hard, glossy finish.

This heatless enamel can be applied to plastic (such as our lampshade), glass, metal, clay (fired or unfired), and wood. You can use it to decorate tiles—for holding hot dishes or for covering part of your bathroom wall. You can use it to make beautiful jewelry (see page 85). A lampshade makes an especially attractive enamel project, for the light shining through the colors will make them glow vividly.

Various manufacturers produce all-inclusive enameling kits, but you can also buy the items separately. To make a lampshade similar to the one shown here, you'll need:

Liquid enamel. This is a plastic material that is available in colorless form and also with colors already added to it.

Hardener. This is mixed with the plastic in a proportion specified by the maker.

Colors. These come in liquid form and are added to the mixture of enamel and hardener.

A measuring cup, for mixing plastic and hardener, and *aluminum foil cups* for mixing enamel and colors.

Mixing sticks, for spreading the enamel.

Cleaning fluid, a type especially designed for use with cold enamel.

A plastic lampshade. This can be purchased in a department store.

Black braid. About 30 feet of lacing cord was needed for a lamp about 18 inches in diameter.

Glue. Use the kind that won't corrode plastic.

You will also need: a *chinagraph pencil*, some *paper*, *cellophane tape*, a *toothpick*, *scissors*, and some *newspaper* to protect the work surface.

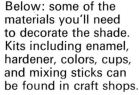

Left: the warm glow of this colorful lampshade helps to make dining together a festive occasion. A new kind of enamel, which goes on without heat, makes it easy for you to create a shade like this one.

Below: some of the materials you'll need to decorate the shade. Kits including enamel, hardener, colors, cups, and mixing sticks can be found in craft shops.

Above: tracing the design onto the shade. Draw petals, etc., on paper, cut them out, and tape them carefully to the underside of the shade.

Below: applying glue to part of the design. Glue only a small part at a time, and immediately apply the braid before the glue has a chance to dry.

Technique

As we have proved, a beginner can make a very handsome enameled lampshade with this new, heatless enamel. But we do advise you to "play around" with the enamel before you get started on a large project such as this one. Buy some small, inexpensive jewelry findings (the metal parts) and practice applying enamel to these. You'll soon acquire the knack of handling enamel and can confidently embark on the lampshade.

1. If the plastic lampshade is very smooth and shiny, roughen it slightly with fine sandpaper so that the enamel will adhere.

2. Draw your design on paper. (If you'd like more design ideas, look for books on *art nouveau* in a library or bookstore.) Decide which colors you want to use. Enamel colors can be mixed to make various shades. When you have decided on colors and design, you are ready to draw the design on the shade. Make sure that you have divided the shade into equal sections to accommodate each motif. Cut out the different parts of the design and place the shapes on the underside of the shade. Attach them with cellophane tape and trace the outlines with a chinagraph pencil. By using the same pattern for each flower or leaf you'll ensure that all of them will be the same size.

3. Apply glue to the drawn lines. Outline one flower or leaf segment at a time (see middle photograph on this page). Cut lengths of braid to go around each outline and keep them handy in separate piles.

4. Apply braid to the glued lines. Do this very carefully, making sure that the braid is firmly glued along its entire length. The braid will serve as a border to the colors, and any gaps between cord and shade will allow the wet colors to run into each other. Make sure that the glue has dried thoroughly

Left: applying braid to make the outline of a leaf. Make sure that the braid is stuck down along its entire length, as enamel will run through gaps.

Left: mixing the enamel. The foil cup contains the mixture of plastic, hardener, and green color. After mixing, allow the enamel to set for an hour until it acquires a gel-like consistency.

Below: spreading the enamel over the design areas. Allowing the enamel to thicken to a gel-like consistency helps to keep it from running down the shade.

before you begin enameling. Allow at least two hours—the longer, the better.

5. Mix the enamel, hardener, and colors according to the manufacturer's instructions. (In the case of already-colored enamel, of course, you will need only to mix the enamel with the hardener.) Mix one color at a time (about half a fluid ounce will cover a fairly large area—for example, the blue area on the top of the shade). Test the enamel on a piece of waxed paper or on a small jewelry finding, to make sure it is the right color. Because parts of the shade have a vertical slope, you will need to let the enamel thicken slightly before applying it to the shade. Leave it for about one hour or so, until it is about the consistency of thick honey. (Some manufacturers produce a thicker enamel especially suited to this kind of project.) When you have applied about half of one color of enamel, mix your next color and let it start to thicken for use later.

6. Using a mixing stick or wooden spatula, apply the enamel to the shade. Gradually

Left: nearly all the enamel has been applied. Watching for any drips and removing thick accumulations of enamel is an important part of the process.

Below: the finished lampshade. The top view shows how the shade was divided into four equal parts for the design. A coat of clear enamel can be applied to the white areas.

push the enamel out to fill in the braided area. To get it well into the edges, use something with a sharp point, such as a toothpick. Even though the enamel has thickened slightly, it will still tend to run down the shade. You must keep a watchful eye on it for a few hours after applying it. Don't do any enameling before going out shopping, or going to bed; for when you return to it you may find that enamel has accumulated at the lower edges of the motifs. Some accumulation will inevitably occur, but this can be removed with the head of a pin. Try to make the enamel an even thickness.

7. When you have finished applying the colored enamel, you can, if you wish, apply a thin coat of uncolored enamel to the white areas of the shade to give a gloss to them. Use a brush and apply the enamel in a liquid state. Watch for drips.

8. Clean the measuring cup and your hands (if necessary) with the cleaning fluid.

9. Allow the lampshade to dry for about a week in a warm dry room. Once the enamel has dried thoroughly, it can safely be used over a large lightbulb. Attach the light fixture and hang the lamp from the ceiling.

More Cold Enamel

A few of the limitless effects you can get using cold enamel are shown in the picture below. Enamel jewelry seems to stay popular year in and year out, and you'll find that your enameled rings, cuff links, pendants, and keychains make very welcome gifts.

You can easily make a design using "strings" or "blobs" of a second color. Simply drip the enamel onto a sheet of waxed paper and let it dry for about 24 hours. Then apply the background color to the finding. Carefully peel the paper from the partly-dried piece of enamel and set this piece into the wet enamel. The two enamels will fuse together in drying. Interesting effects can be obtained by swirling the second color directly into the wet base coat.

You'll find it convenient to place jewelry findings on an inverted paper cup while applying the enamel. Small findings can be stuck into Styrofoam or placed on a strip of adhesive tape to keep them steady.

Cloisonné work, such as the narrow brooch in the left of the picture, is also easy to do. First cover the article with a base coat of enamel and let it dry slightly for about 3 hours. Insert copper wire bent into your chosen design. Allow a few more hours of drying, then fill the separate areas formed by the wire with the various colors. It's a good idea to practice this technique on a larger item, such as a tile, first.

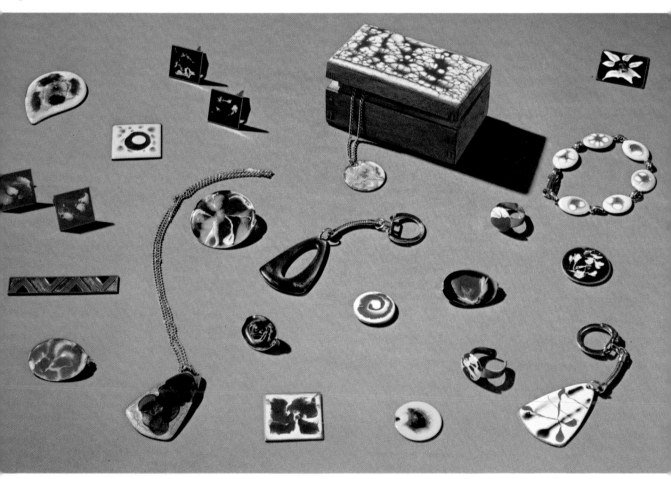

A selection of jewelry and a jewel box, showing a few of the varied and attractive effects that can be achieved by working in colorful heatless enamel

Many artists these days are discovering the possibilities of string and wire. Some of their creations are really dazzling—such as the enormous silver-wire sculpture that glistens in the entrance to the Pan Am Building in New York.

There's something almost hypnotically fascinating about string art—the way straight lines can be formed into curved and twisting shapes. And, happily, you can create intriguing and colorful string sculpture with very little expense. Of course, you need to plan your design carefully—the ones shown opposite were done by someone with a bit of experience, and they used a slightly more advanced technique (described on page 89). But once you begin to get the feel for the materials you can create equally beautiful designs with string. If you enjoyed geometry at school, you'll find string art irresistible. If you *didn't* like geometry—give it a try, anyway! You may surprise yourself.

Start with the simple but effective design shown below. To make it, you'll need:

Wooden board, such as plywood, about $\frac{3}{4}$ of an inch thick, and about 1 foot square.

Fabric to cover the board. This should be fairly closely woven.

Colored string in two different colors, about 33 feet of each color.

Drawing paper, about $\frac{1}{2}$ an inch smaller than the board.

A screw or bolt, about $2\frac{1}{2}$ inches long. Ideally, you should use a bolt and nut. This means drilling a hole in the wood, inserting the nut, and screwing the bolt into it. This will be very strong. Or you can use a pointed screw designed for use with wood. This has the advantage of not requiring you to drill a hole first, and no nut is needed. It is probably strong enough for this purpose. For an extra-strong sculpture, use the bolt and nut, and add a washer.

Silver-colored nails, about 1 inch long, with small heads. You'll need about 60 of these. You'll also need some *carpet tacks*, a *hammer*, a *screwdriver*, a *ruler*, a *pencil*, a pair of *compasses*, and *scissors*.

Left: a dramatic display of string art, made by the hole-threading technique. Somewhat easier is the pretty "sunburst" sculpture shown below. Materials for this string sculpture are illustrated at right.

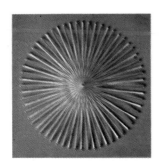

Above: securing the fabric on the back of the board with carpet tacks. Take care to pull the fabric taut in both directions and make neat corners.

Above: drawing the design on paper. Fix the compasses at about a 5½-inch radius, and divide the circle into an even number of lines.

Below: inserting the bolt through the cross-cuts in the paper and the fabric. Either a wood screw or a bolt, nut and washer may be used.

Technique

1. Find the center point of the board, using a ruler, and make a dot at that point. If you are using a bolt and nut for the center support, drill a hole at that point, and chip a small piece from the underside to make a shallow depression. Insert the nut (and washer) here, but do not insert the bolt yet. If you are using a wood screw, make a hole by screwing it into the wood and then removing it.

2. Cover the board with your fabric. Pull it taut in all directions, and make neat corners. Fasten it on the underside with carpet tacks.

3. Now make your design on the paper. Using your compasses, draw a circle about 10 inches in diameter. Divide the circle into 56 evenly spaced lines, radiating out from the center. (You can use more or fewer lines, but it must be an even number.)

4. Make a tiny cross cut in the center of the paper (like this: +) and fold the four corners back. Make a similar cut in the fabric, but do not fold the corners back.

5. Position the paper on the board so that the two cross cuts are superimposed, and attach it to the fabric with cellophane tape.

6. Insert screw or bolt in hole. The edges of the fabric will be pushed down into the hole as you do this. About $1\frac{1}{4}$ inches of the shank of the screw will be sticking up out of the board, and on this you will wind your string.

7. Hammer the nails into the board through the design, putting a nail at each point where a line crosses the edge of the circle. Hammer each nail in until only $\frac{3}{8}$ of an inch remains above the surface.

8. Remove the paper by simply ripping it from one corner. (But check first to make sure you've positioned all the nails correctly.)

9. Now you are ready to string. Start with the blue thread—or whatever color you prefer to have underneath. Make a slip knot and fasten this around the center screw. (To make sure it doesn't come undone, you can apply a dab of clear nail polish or glue.) Trim the loose end. Pull the string toward one of

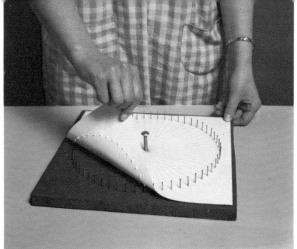

Above: hammering the nails in a circular pattern. We used silver-colored nails for this sculpture, but you may prefer to use brass ones instead.

Above: ripping the paper pattern away once all the nails have been hammered into place. Make sure that the nails are positioned properly.

the nails, and pass it around the nail from left to right and back to the center screw. Go around the screw from left to right. Now wind the string around the second nail to the right of the starting nail, again from left to right. Continue winding around each alternate nail until you return to the starting point. You cross the string over itself each time you return to the center. Each center loop goes on top of the previous one, creating a raised, three-dimensional effect. Keep the string taut at all times, as a loose string here and there will spoil the effect of your design.

10. Now join the yellow string (or other second color) to the blue, so that the knot occurs at the center screw. Wind the string as before, going around the alternate empty nails. Finish off by knotting the string around the screw. This knot should fit neatly just under the head of the screw. If there is still a little space, you can push the screw a bit farther into the board.

With this basic technique of winding string around nails, you can work many variations. But you can greatly enlarge your design scope by using a different method of string sculpture. In the method used to create the designs in the opening picture no nails are used. Instead, you bore holes in the wood and thread string through them. You can create very intricate patterns this way. Paint the wood to make an attractive background. Plan the design carefully, as it's difficult to get rid of a hole once you've made it!

Above: starting to wind the blue string around the screw and nails. Keeping the string taut while winding helps give professional-looking results.

Below: the completed string sculpture. Once you've done this simple design, you should be able to create your own original patterns.

Flower Pressing

12

Collecting flowers, pressing them, and using them to make lovely decorations for your home is a satisfying and inexpensive pastime. It requires a minimum of fuss and materials, and offers a lot of pleasure. Your family can join in this activity—helping to gather wild flowers on country walks, and, later, arranging the dried flowers to decorate lampshades, trays, and other objects. But do remember that today many wild flowers are protected, and fines for picking them can be severe. So check with your state Department of Conservation or Forestry before setting out.

Your own flower garden—if you've got one—can supply you with flowers for pressing. The pretty blossoms of spring and summer can be preserved in dried form to brighten many winters.

The serving cart shown opposite was purchased plain and decorated with a spray of pansies, ferns, and some delicate wild flowers. A sheet of glass laid on top of the arrangement protects the flowers and gives the cart an easy-to-clean surface.

Materials you'll need to decorate a serving cart with pressed flowers include:
White mounting board, the same size as the top of the cart.
A piece of glass, the same size as the board.
Glue, of the clear-drying variety (important).
A toothpick or pin, for spreading the glue, and some *waxed paper.*
A paper butterfly (optional) from a package of transfer decorations.
A flower press. You can easily make one of these, using: two pieces of stiff *cardboard* (about 8 by 12 inches), two lengths of *ribbon* (each about 1 yard long), and some *blotting paper,* or newspaper.

Cut slits in the cardboard and insert the ribbon as shown in the drawing below. Take the press with you on trips to the country.

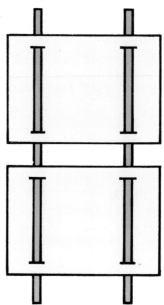

Right: a spray of flowers gives a graceful and colorful touch to a serving cart. Finally, a sheet of glass protects the arrangement.

Left: this drawing shows the inside of a flower press, opened flat. Make one and take it with you when you go out in the country to gather flowers.

Far left: collecting flowers for pressing can rapidly become an activity that the whole family can enjoy.

$\mathcal{T}$echnique

To press the flowers, first open your flower press and lay a sheet of blotting paper on one side of the press (or you can use several sheets of newspaper, but make sure it's old newspaper and that the print won't come off onto the flowers). Lay some of the flowers on the paper, without allowing them to over-lap. Select flowers of roughly the same thickness for this layer, and group other sizes together for other layers. The important thing is to have even pressure on all the flowers. Thick blossoms will lift the paper away from any delicate blossoms in the same layer, causing these to wither.

In the case of flowers having thick centers and delicate petals (such as daisies), you will need to insert some padding. Cut a small piece of blotting paper to cover the blossom, and cut a hole in it the size of the flower's center. Lay this over the petals. Add more pieces until the paper is level with the center. This extra paper will dry the petals, which otherwise would not get enough pressure. Cover the flowers with blotting paper (or newspaper). Add other layers of flowers and paper, finishing with a layer of paper. Close the press and tie the ribbons tightly (if you are out in the country) to begin the drying process right away. At home, lay heavy books on top of the press and leave them there for at least a month. Don't open the press during this time, as this will prevent the flowers from drying properly.

When the flowers have dried for a month, you are ready to use them on your serving cart.

1. Open the press, carefully removing the layers of paper and padding, and select the flowers and leaves you want to use in your design.

2. Arrange and rearrange the flowers on the

Left: examining the dried flowers and selecting those suitable for decorating the top of the serving cart.

Right: arranging the chosen flowers on the white mounting board. Take your time, and arrange and rearrange the flowers until you achieve a design that really pleases you.

Below: applying glue to the backs of the flowers, using a toothpick. Each flower is placed on the board right after gluing.

board until you make a design that pleases you.

3. Begin gluing down the flowers. Pick up a flower, lay it upside down on a piece of waxed paper, and spread the glue on it, using a toothpick or pin. Carefully place the flower on the board and gently press your finger over its entire surface to make sure that it is stuck down firmly. Repeat this with all other flowers and leaves in the design. (If you like, add a paper butterfly; the one in our picture came from a package of transfers.)

4. When the glue has dried thoroughly, place the card on the cart top and lay the piece of glass over it.

5. If you intend to keep this design permanently, protect it from dust and spills by filling in the space around the edge of the glass with glue.

You can use these same techniques to decorate a tray. For this project, it's a good idea to substitute something like plexiglass for the

93

glass top, as it is lightweight and unbreakable.

When you have pressed your flowers you will probably find that their original colors have faded noticeably. In some cases, the softer colors will be pleasing and quite suitable for your project. But if you want brighter colors, give nature a boost with a little paint, after the flowers have dried thoroughly.

Use watercolors, adding a little detergent with the tip of your brush to make the paint adhere to the flowers. (Some plants are more water-repellent than others and will require more detergent in the paint.) Lay the painted flowers to dry in the open air—don't apply heat as this may shrivel them.

To strengthen very fragile petals—and give them added color—glue them to a piece of paper of the desired color. Use clear glue. After the glue has dried, cut carefully around the petals, so that no paper is visible around them. The color of the paper will show through the petals.

Above: placing the board, with its arrangement of dried flowers, on the top of the serving cart.
Below left: placing the glass on top of the flowers. If the design is to be permanent, it's a good idea to add glue to the space around the glass.
Below right: the decorated serving cart, ready to help you entertain with style.

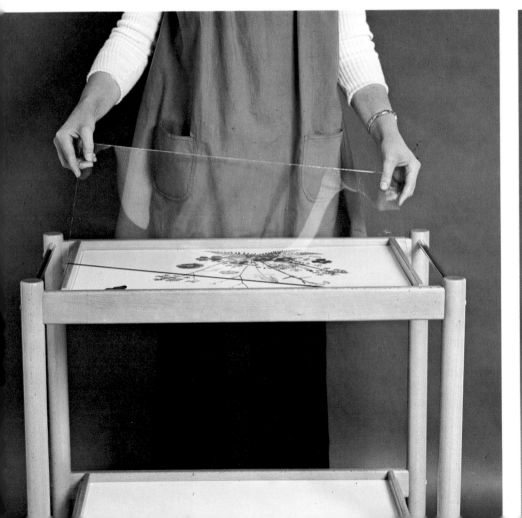

More Flower Pressing

Pressed flowers lend themselves to many other decorations. Among the simplest are place cards for a party. Use plain white or colored cards (you can buy these, or cut them from construction paper) measuring about $4\frac{1}{2}$ by 5 inches opened flat. Fold each card down the center (lengthwise) so that it will stand. Print one guest's name on each card, and when the ink is dry glue the flower in position. If you want to keep the cards for future use, cut pieces of plastic film large enough to cover one side of a card, plus a little extra to tuck under the edges. Lay this smoothly over the card, fold the excess under and fasten it with strips of transparent tape.

Tall grasses give a distinctive touch to a purchased plastic lampshade. Choose grasses of different heights, as shown in the picture. If some of the grasses have rather sturdy heads, this will help to give a three-dimensional effect. First tape the grasses in place with a bit of transparent tape and adjust their positions as necessary. Glue each one in place. When all the glue has dried, remove the tape and apply lacquer to the shade. The aerosol type of lacquer is easy to use, but the kind you apply with a brush will also do.

Above: pretty place cards for a children's party, easily made with pressed flowers.

Left: this flower picture uses blooms that have been painted after pressing, to restore their original colors.

Right: a smart modern lampshade, embellished with dried grasses. Thick stems should be pared down on one side (use a razor blade) so that they will lie flat.

A Découpage Tray

13

If you have a taste for elegance, you'll enjoy decoupage. Basically, decoupage—which is derived from the French word "couper," "to cut"—consists in decorating an object with pictures that are carefully cut out and glued into place. The entire surface is covered with many coats of varnish to achieve a satin-smooth surface.

The technique of decoupage was developed in the 18th century when elaborately decorated Oriental lacquer ware was in vogue. The genuine article was expensive and scarce, and soon imitations, made with cutout designs, began to appear. Then considered "poor man's lacquer," decoupage is now valued for its own sake. All sorts of useful objects—from matchboxes to chests of drawers—can be made into charming conversation pieces with decoupage.

An extremely rewarding craft, decoupage is also a rather demanding one. You need a bit of imagination and a feeling for design, perseverance in finding appropriate prints for your work, and lots of patience. Many coats of varnish must be applied, allowed to dry, and sanded, before a project is complete. But if you don't mind taking pains over a task, you'll get gratifying results.

The handsome tray shown opposite was made by a beginner. You can make one

Left: a beginner proudly displays her first effort in the art of decoupage—a handsome tray painted black and decorated with Japanese figures. Many coats of varnish give the tray a smooth finish.

Right: the materials used in making the tray. The increasing popularity of this craft is indicated by the growing number of companies offering materials for it—including a wide range of prints.

similar to it. By way of materials you'll need:
The tray. We used an inexpensive, imitation-wood tray, available in department and hardware stores.
Colored prints. Ours came from a second-hand book, but you could also use pictures from a magazine, wallpaper samples, Christmas cards, or other greeting cards. Decoupage is now so popular that some companies are even producing prints especially designed for the craft. Some of these prints are left uncolored so that you can color them yourself. In choosing prints from sources other than these decoupage suppliers, be careful to choose paper that

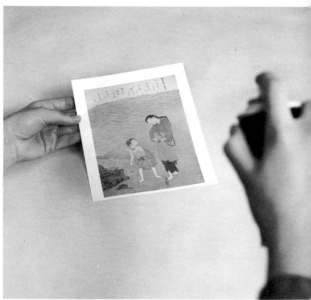

Above: after a thorough sanding to remove the old finish, the tray is then given two coats of black paint.

Above right: applying aerosol sealer to the print to keep the colors in it from running into the varnish.

Technique

isn't too thick. The thicker the paper, the more difficult it will be to obtain a smooth surface on your work.

Manicure scissors and a *razor blade* for cutting out the prints. Put the razor blade in a holder before attempting to use it.

Sealer. This is a plastic spray in a can.

Paint, either oil-based or water-based for the background color of the tray.

Brushes: a 1-inch brush for painting, a 2-inch brush for varnishing, and a small brush for gluing.

Glue. A white glue is most useful.

A roller, for smoothing cutouts after gluing.

Varnish and *mineral spirits.* The choice of a varnish is fairly important. For best results use a slow-drying varnish, as this kind is more durable than the fast-drying kind. Either a glossy or a flat varnish can be used. The mineral spirits are for thinning the varnish.

Wet-and-dry sandpaper, both medium-fine and extra-fine grain, and a *block* for holding it.

Steel wool, the 0000 variety.

Paste wax, to give the object a gloss finish.

You will also need a *sponge,* a *cloth* for waxing, and some *waxed paper.*

1. Sand the tray all over, using extra-fine sandpaper, until the old finish is completely removed. Then rub it lightly with 0000 steel wool to achieve a very smooth surface.

2. Paint the tray with the background color you have chosen. If you use a water-based paint, apply sealer before painting. With an oil-based paint, no sealer is necessary. When the paint is thoroughly dry, sand the tray with extra-fine sandpaper, and apply a second coat of paint. When this has dried, sand again and apply sealer. (*Note:* use aerosol sprays only in a well-ventilated room.) The tray is now ready for the cutouts to be stuck onto it.

3. Spray the print with sealer. This sets the color and gives the print more body, making it easier to cut. If there is printed material on the back of the print, check after applying the sealer to see if the printing is visible on the right side. If the material does show through, coat the wrong side with matt black paint, and seal this surface when dry.

4. Cut out the prints. Hold the scissors with the blades curved to the right, and carefully feed the paper into the scissors. (Note: if you

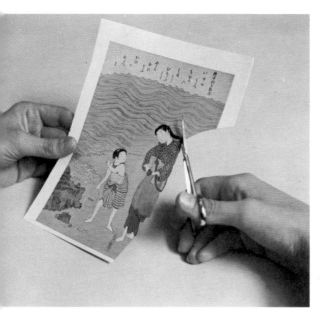

Left: cutting out the print. Notice that the scissor blades are held so that they curve away from the figure. The left hand feeds the paper into the scissors.

Right: face down on a sheet of paper, the cut-out is given a coat of white glue.

Below: glued into place, the cutout is covered with a piece of waxed paper, and pressed flat with the aid of a roller.

Above: applying varnish to the tray. A good finish will require at least 10 coats—each of them being allowed to dry for about 24 hours.

are left-handed, hold the scissors with the blades curved to the left.) The hand holding the scissors should not move except for opening and closing the blades. To remove inside portions, you can use a razor-blade.

5. Arrange the cutouts on the tray until you get a pleasing design.

6. Having decided on a design, you are now ready to apply the glue. Thin the glue with a few drops of water (if it is water-soluble) and brush it all over the cutout. Place the cutout on the tray and cover it with a sheet of waxed paper. Using the roller, press the cutout firmly and evenly onto the surface. Remove the paper and check the edges of the cutout for any excess glue. Remove this with a clean sponge dipped in warm water. A bit of vinegar on the sponge, or on a Q-tip, will take care of stubborn areas of glue. When you have finished, allow the tray to dry thoroughly.

7. Apply the first coat of varnish, letting it

100

flow easily and evenly onto the surface. Check for hairs that may have come from the brush. Pick these up using the brush held flat. Watch also for runs and drips, and brush them out if they appear. Allow the tray to dry for 24 hours. Repeat the varnishing at least 10 times, allowing 24 hours' drying time between each coat.

8. When the cutouts are *well covered* with varnish, so that you can no longer feel any sharp edges, but only gentle "slopes," around them, you can begin to sand. (You may find it necessary to do a little light sanding *before* this stage if any dust or air bubbles have caught in the varnish. We did a little sanding after the sixth coat in order to get rid of these. But be very careful not to sand down to the prints.) Use wet-and-dry extra-fine sandpaper, soaking wet. You may find it easier to apply the water directly to the tray. Wrap the sandpaper around the block for ease in handling, and sand with even strokes. The surface over the cutouts will be very slightly higher than the surface over the base.

Carefully go over the entire surface, taking care not to sand too deeply over the prints. When the surface is fairly smooth, wipe the milky waste off with a damp sponge and allow the tray to dry. You will probably need to apply another coat of varnish, sand again, and repeat the process several times, in order to get a good finish. It's impossible to state exactly how many coats of varnish and how many sandings will be necessary. Each decoupage project is different. Keep a sharp eye on your work and test it frequently with your fingertips. If you think you may be getting too close to the prints, stop sanding, and apply another coat of varnish. Keep repeating the varnishing and sanding process until the surface is completely level.

9. To give the surface a satiny finish, rub it with extra-fine 0000 steel wool. Use small pieces and rub with a circular motion. Continue until the surface is perfectly smooth.

10. Apply wax polish very sparingly with a slightly damp cloth. Allow the wax to dry, and buff it with a soft cloth to obtain a sheen.

Left: moistened with water, the tray is given a sanding with extra-fine sandpaper, wrapped around a block for ease in handling. The slight bulges over the cutouts are leveled, but without damaging the cutouts themselves.

Left: a small piece of grade 0000 steel wool completes the smoothing.

Right: applying wax polish with a soft cloth, using a circular motion, gives the tray a professional-looking sheen.

More Découpage

You can see the versatility of decoupage in these pictures. Dainty boxes, such as the ones shown opposite, are among the most popular projects. The board and bottle shown below use both collage and decoupage techniques, and were decorated by a 10-year-old girl.

The cheese board (opposite) makes a charming and useful gift. Buy a plain, unfinished wooden board, sand it well until it is smooth, apply a sealer, and sand it again. To bring out the grain and give it a rich pine color, apply two coats of a wood dye. Apply the print, varnish, sand, and polish as for the tray described in the preceding pages.

Decoupage under glass (below) is an interesting—and easy—variation on the basic technique. Choose a dish with a flat bottom. Cut out and seal the print. Apply glue to its *front* surface, and immediately press it into place on the underside of the dish. Press out any excess glue with your fingers, looking through the bottom of the dish as you do so. Make sure that the cutout is stuck evenly over its entire surface. Remove excess glue with a damp sponge. Let the glue dry for several hours. Apply sealer over the entire bottom of the dish. This will keep the paint from running under the print. When the sealer has dried, apply paint in your chosen color to the bottom of the dish, covering the cutout and the glass. Let this dry and then apply a second coat if necessary. Finally, cut a circle of felt to fit the bottom of the dish. Apply glue to the painted surface and stick the felt firmly to the glued surface.

Below: decoupage under glass. This pretty dish involves no varnishing. The print was backed with sealer, a coat of white paint, and a piece of felt.

Below: magazine cutouts were overlapped in a collage for this wall-decoration and vase. Orange shellac gives a mellow "antique" look.

Right: the decoration for this attractive cheese board came from a shop selling various inexpensive prints.

Below: boxes are useful for holding all sorts of things, and you can make them beautiful with a decoupage finish. A special book deserves a special cover: here, too, decoupage provides it.

The Art of Polished Stones
14

Some of the prettiest jewelry around these days is made not with diamonds and rubies, but with pebbles! The beautiful colors and patterns in quartz, agate, and other plentiful stones, emerge readily with tumble polishing. The resulting smooth, shiny stones can be used in rings, bracelets, or any other ornament you desire. On the following pages, we show you how to make a simple but eye-catching pendant.

If you don't want to get involved with polishing stones yourself, you can buy already-polished pebbles from a lapidary supplier—a shop specializing in rocks and equipment for collectors. The dealer can supply you not only with polished stones but also with materials for making them into jewelry.

But you may find the shop and its wares so fascinating that you'll walk out with a tumbler under your arm. A tumbler is a small machine containing a barrel in which stones are rotated, along with water and an abrasive, until they acquire a high luster. (Not all stones polish well; a book or pamphlet for collectors will tell you which to look for and which to discard.) Tumbling a load of pebbles takes a total of about 18 or 19 days (with the motor running constantly); seven days with a coarse grit, seven with a finer grit, and four or five with a polishing compound. You should have an extra barrel just for polishing, as any grit that gets into the barrel at this stage will spoil the polishing.

One thing to bear in mind if you're considering buying a tumbler is that it will make a bit of noise. It's best to keep it in the basement or garage, out of earshot.

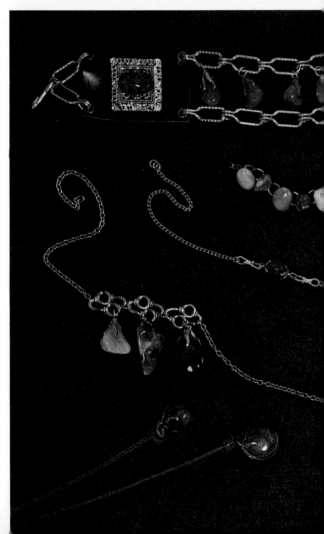

Left: an assortment of pebbles, just as they were gathered on a day at the beach, before being placed in the tumbler for polishing.

Right: the same pebbles, polished and shining, as they look after several weeks in the tumbler.

Below: a collection of belts, necklaces, and bracelets, all using polished pebbles.

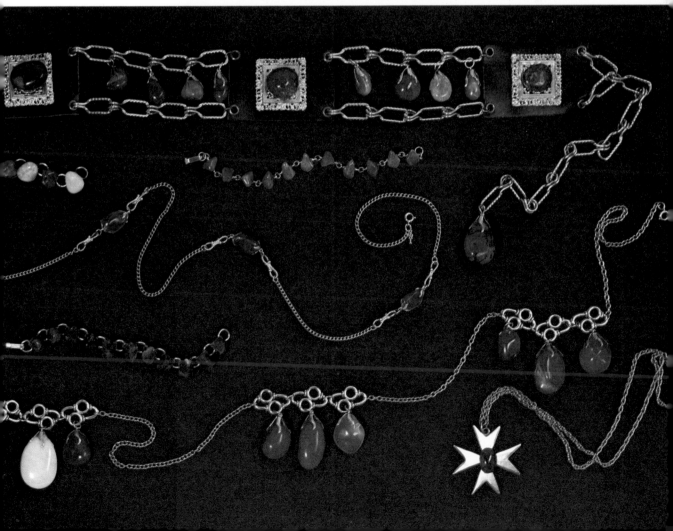

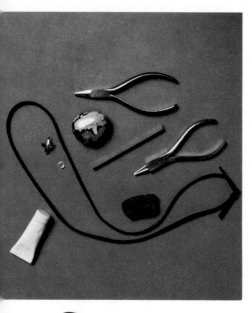

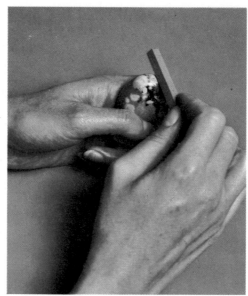

Far left: the materials you'll need to make a pendant on a leather thong. The stone is a flinty pebble.

Left: roughening the tip of the stone with a silicone carbide stick to make it more receptive to the glue.

Right: applying glue with a matchstick to the bell cap finding.

Technique

The pendant shown on these pages uses some of the basic techniques used in most pebble jewelry.

Besides the stone (we used a flinty pebble) you'll need:

A bell cap finding and a large *jump ring*. These and other findings (metal jewelry parts) can be purchased from a craft shop or a lapidary supplier.

Pliers, both round-nosed and flat-nosed.

Clear adhesive, such as epoxy resin.

A leather thong, about one yard in length.

A silicone carbide stick, acetone, a soft *cloth,* some *matchsticks,* and some *modeling clay.*

1. Press the metal bell cap onto the top of the stone, molding it to the shape of the stone.

2. Rub the top of the stone with the silicone carbide stick. This will roughen the surface so that the adhesive has a better surface to cling to.

3. Clean the stone with the acetone. Avoid touching the part of the stone that will be attached to the finding, as oil from your fingers will impair the bonding of the stone and the finding.

4. Using a matchstick, apply adhesive to the bell cap. Put another small blob on the roughened part of the stone. Press the molded bell cap firmly onto the stone.

5. Set the stone upright in the modeling clay. Using a clean matchstick, remove excess glue from the stone. Leave the stone in the modeling clay for 24 hours so that the glue can dry and harden.

6. Thread the jump ring through the eye of the bell cap. Close and tighten the ring with the flat-nosed pliers.

7. Thread the leather thong through the ring. Tie the ends in a knot or bow. The pendant is now ready to wear.

You can use this basic technique in making bracelets, earrings, and other kinds of jewelry. Instead of leather you could use a chain or a wire collar for your pendant (see page 35). If you want to make a pair of cuff links or earrings and find that you haven't got two matching stones, your lapidary supplier can cut one in half for you.

You'll find that polished pebbles have many other beautiful uses besides jewelry. In fact, if you do your own polishing, you'll have a hard time making enough jewelry to use up the stones. Select only the outstanding ones for jewelry, and use the rest in other ways. Put them in a glass bowl or a large brandy glass as a table decoration. Better yet, use them in a mosaic (see pages 18 through 25).

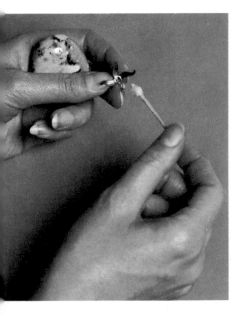

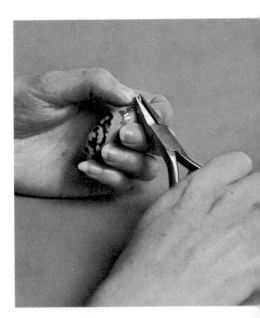

Above center: after you've glued on the finding, set the stone in modeling clay to keep it upright, and leave it to dry completely. This will take 24 hours.

Above right: next, insert the jump ring in the bell cap. Use the pliers to close the jump ring firmly in readiness for the next step in the craft—threading.

Below: this picture shows that final step. Here we used a leather thong to thread the pendant, but you could use a fine chain—the choice is up to you.

Right: the finished pendant—a perfect accessory to complement a sweater, as here, or a simple dress.

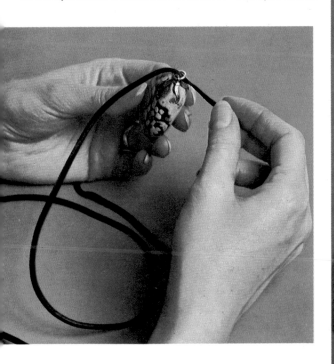

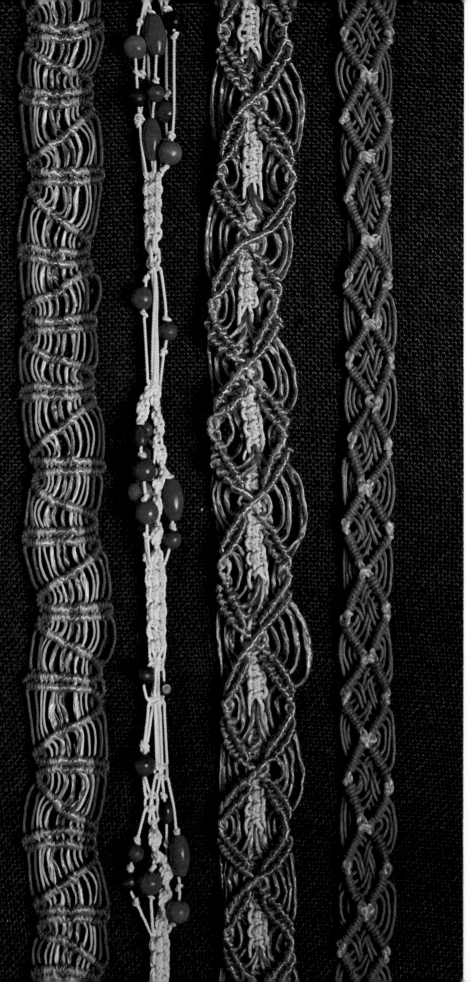

Left: these four eye-catching belts are not as difficult as they look. Instructions for the belts—designated, from left to right, B, C, D, E—begin on page 113.

Below: begin learning macramé by making this simple Belt A in three colors. Instructions for Belt A are given on the next few pages.

Below right: materials you'll need in making the red, blue, and green belt. The board should be of soft wood that will take nails easily.

The simplest dress acquires a lot of chic when you add a colorful macramé belt. You can make one yourself. Macramé is all done with knots—varying combinations of a few basic knots that you can learn quite easily. Some macramé designs are rather complex and require a bit of experience, but you can make the belts shown here with only a little practice. In the following pages, we show you how. Later, you can embark on other projects: bags, vests, jewelry, and wall-hangings. Macramé is exotic, and yet modern and informal. No wonder it has become, in the past few years, one of the most popular crafts.

To make Belt A, shown in the picture below, you'll need:

Natural cotton cord, about $\frac{1}{8}$ of an inch thick, cut into four lengths, each one eight times the length of the finished article. For example, to make a 28-inch belt, you will need four lengths about 19 feet long. Using several different colors will help you to follow the diagrams and will also result in

a more interesting belt. You can buy cotton cord already dyed, or you can buy white cord and dye it yourself, using a cold-water dye. But you needn't confine yourself to cotton cord in your macrame work. Yarn—especially rug yarn—nylon cord, or twine can be used to create a variety of textures. The one thing to remember is to choose yarn or string that will give a firm knot that won't slip.

A board, on which to anchor your work. You can use a wooden board, preferably a soft wood that will take pins easily. If the wood is hard, pad it with a towel. Very stiff cardboard can serve as a board.

Two nails, or *pins,* or some *adhesive tape,* for fastening the work to the board.

A buckle. We've used a simple, loop-type buckle, which goes particularly well with macrame, but you'll find many other kinds at a good notions counter. (Or, you can simply tie the cords together.)

A pair of scissors and a *tape measure* are the other materials you'll need for this belt.

Left: how to arrange your macramé work in making a belt. Fasten the buckle with several pins or nails (or with adhesive tape) so that it won't slip around. Spread the loose cords out—half on your right and half on your left. This will help to keep them from tangling.

Right: the diagrams on the next two pages show you, step by step, how to make the simple belt shown on this page. Use a different color scheme if you prefer, but if you use three colors, arranged as shown, you'll find the diagrams easy to follow.

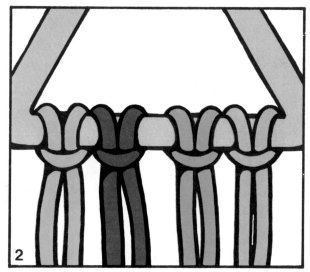

Technique

Belt A: Only two basic knots are needed in making this attractive macramé belt. They're easy to do, as you'll realize once you begin working. Macramé diagrams look complicated at first, but when you begin to knot, you'll find they make sense. (Our instructions are for two blue cords, one green cord, and one red cord, but you may substitute other colors if you wish.)

1. First attach one part of the buckle to the board, using adhesive tape or a couple of nails hammered in at a slight angle.

2. Take one of the blue cords, double it, and slip the loop under the crossbar of the buckle (as shown with the red cord in Diagram 1). Then bring the ends over the bar and slip them through the loop. Pull the knot tight. This is called the *lark's head,* or *hitching knot,* and is one of the knots commonest in macrame. Make three more lark's heads with the remaining cords (Diagram 2). You now have eight working cords.

3. Now take the left-hand four cords and make a left-hand square knot. Study Diagram 3 and you'll see how to make this knot. Notice that the two center cords (of the group of four) serve as carrier cords, while you use the outer two cords to make the knot. Pull the knot fairly tight; the diagram shows the cords loose for clarity only.

4. Make a right-hand square knot using the right-hand four cords, as in Diagram 3. The *square knot* (which usually means a left-hand square knot, unless a right-hand knot is specified) is another of the knots most frequently used in macramé.

5. Now, using the center four cords, make a square knot as shown in Diagram 4.

6. With the two inner blue cords make two sideways lark's heads around the other blue cords, as shown in Diagram 5. You have now completed one pattern of the belt. Repeat the pattern—three square knots,

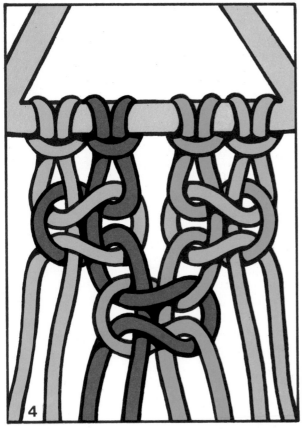

two lark's heads—until the belt is the desired length, finishing with a center square knot and the two lark's heads.

7. Make a single knot in each cord (Diagram 6), leaving enough space between the last knots of the pattern and these finishing knots for you to be able to wrap the cord once around the bar of the buckle.

8. Wrap each cord around the buckle and tack it into place with needle and thread. Trim the ends.

Now that you've made one macramé belt, you know that this craft is easier than it looks. Perhaps you'll want to try a few more belts with slightly more intricate patterns. Belts are a good project for building your skill in knotting, because—aside from length—you don't have to worry about size and shaping. Also, you can finish a belt fairly quickly and get a sense of accomplishment in a short time.

The four belts shown in the opening picture give you an idea of the many variations you can make in belts alone.

Belts B and C (shown above right) require the following materials. Belt B: four lengths of string, two in red, and two in yellow; and three lengths of blue plastic-coated twine. (Unless otherwise stated, a "length" is eight times the finished length.) Belt C: three lengths of natural-colored parcel string and a number of wooden beads.

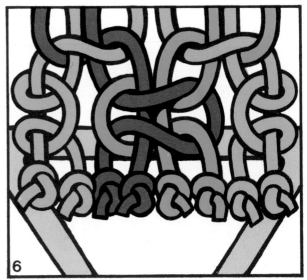

112

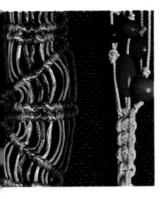

Left: detail of two belts shown in the photograph on page 108. Belt B, at left, uses one knot, done on a leader cord that runs through the design.

Right: diagrams 1 and 2 show you how to make Belt B. A slight curve (shown in the photo) occurs naturally as you continue knotting.

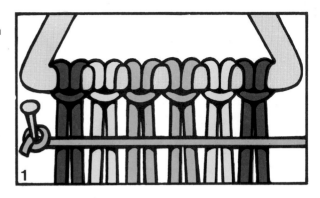

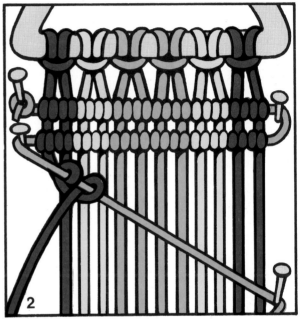

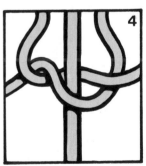

Belt B: Fasten six cords on the buckle, using the lark's head, so that you have 12 working cords.

1. Hammer a nail at the side of the cords as shown in Diagram 1, and tie one end of the extra blue twine around this.

2. Loop each cord over the leader cord, using the *loop knot*, shown in Diagram 2.

3. When you reach the end of the row, put in another nail, and loop the leader cord around it. Make another row of loop knots just below the first.

4. Loop the leader cord around another nail and bring it down at an angle across the working cords as shown in Diagram 2. Continue knotting along the leader cord as shown in the diagram. Two horizontal rows alternating with one slanting row make the pattern. Repeat until the belt is the desired length, finishing with two horizontal rows.

Belt C: This is a "free form" style especially suitable for a tie-belt.

1. Double the three cords to make six working cords. Knot the six cords together about two feet from the looped ends. Fasten this knot to the board.

2. Make a row of five to seven alternating left- and right-hand square knots (Diagram 3), working with the four outside cords and leaving the two inside as carrier cords.

3. Using three cords, make a spiral of *half knots* (shown in Diagram 4).

4. Alongside the spiral, string beads on the other cords, tying knots between beads.

5. Vary the pattern to suit yourself. To finish the belt, knot all the cords together. Cut the loops at the other end. Leave six long unequal cords on each end.

Above: the half knot, or twisting knot, used in Belt C, is simply the first half of a right-hand square knot. When repeated, it twists into a spiral.

Left: the square knot using six cords is also used in Belt C.

113

Above: details of belts D and E from our first photograph. Both belts use the square knot and loop knot. Instructions for Belt D (shown in the diagram) are given in the following caption; instructions for Belt E are given below.

Right: although rather complicated-looking, Belt D consists of only two knots—the square and the loop—plus the beginning row of larks' heads. Study the diagram carefully. It is greatly enlarged and slightly distorted in order to show clearly where each strand goes. Where the two leader cords cross in the center, one makes a loop knot around the other—and around one of the center cords.

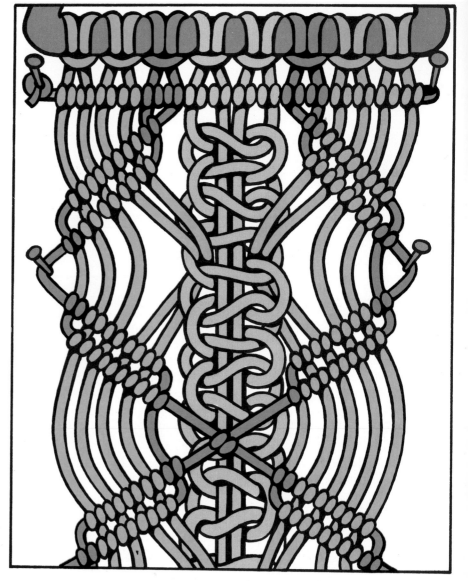

Belt D is more complicated, but if you study the diagram and caption, you'll see that it is made of two knots you already know— the square and the loop. We have varied the pattern slightly from that shown in the photograph, making the belt easier to do, and just as pretty. To make it, you will need four lengths of blue plastic-coated twine and two lengths of green; two lengths of string.
Belt E is similar to Belt D, but somewhat easier. It requires four lengths of red string and two lengths of yellow plastic twine.
1. Attach the cords to the buckle to make 12 cords: four red, four yellow, four red.
2. Tie a square knot with the yellow cords.

3. Pull the two left-hand yellow cords diagonally to the left and tie loop knots (see Belt B) over these two cords. Repeat (reversing the direction) with two right-hand yellow cords.
4. Weave string together as shown in the photograph on page 108.
5. Bend one yellow cord around a pin and tie a loop knot around it with the other yellow cord. Repeat on the other side.
6. Pull the two left-hand yellow cords down toward center and knot red string around them as before. Repeat on other side.
7. Tie a square knot with the yellow cords in the center. This completes the pattern.

More Macramé

If you enjoy making the belts shown in these pages, you'll probably want to move on to more dramatic examples of macramé. A wall-hanging—particularly a bright-colored one against a whitewashed wall—gives a plain room a touch of the exotic. A macramé vest is the perfect foil for a simple dress or pantsuit. A macramé bikini —if you're brave enough to wear it—should make you the seaside sensation.

Mix knots with beads for variety of texture in macramé projects. Dye your own string for more subtle colors than you can buy. Experiment with various kinds of string and yarn. Let your imagination go, and create your own macramé designs.

Above right: this lampshade is made with square knots, linked together by their carrier cords.

Left: this richly patterned wall-hanging is worked on a short stick, from which it is suspended.

Below: two cords knotted together as one give an interesting texture to these macramé curtains.

Right: macrame makes attractive shoulder-bags, such as the smart rust-colored one in our picture.

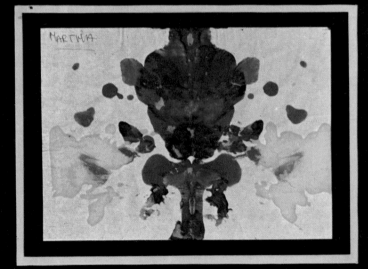

Easy Picture Framing

16

The pleasure of buying a reproduction of your favorite Monet, or taking a photograph of your one-year-old son, or receiving an original painting à la Jackson Pollock from your six-year-old is often followed by a feeling of perplexity: what to do about a frame? Many a favorite picture lies rolled up on a closet shelf because the owner can't decide how to get it up on the wall.

Taking a picture to a professional framer can be an expensive proposition. Attempting to frame it yourself is a tricky business that often produces a lop-sided frame and some bruised fingers. One answer to the problem is *passe-partout*. Literally meaning "goes everywhere," this French phrase also refers to a kind of framing that uses adhesive tape instead of a conventional frame. You simply put glass, picture, mat, and backing together and bind the edges with tape. It's simple, and easy on the pocket as well.

Obviously passe-partout won't do for everything. Some pictures really call for molded frames. But many photos, prints, and drawings show up to good advantage with this simple technique.

You can also use passe-partout without glass, thus cutting expense and bother to the absolute minimum.

Materials you'll need for passe-partout framing include:

Mat paper in a size several inches larger than the picture itself. The width of the mat border can vary enormously, depending on the picture and the kind of frame, but with passe-partout a border of about 1 to $1\frac{1}{2}$ inches is usually desirable. It's also a good idea to allow for a wider margin on the bottom than on the sides and top.

Above: children's drawings and paintings deserve a little attention. You can frame them easily and effectively with a piece of glass and adhesive tape

Left: this group of pictures, which were all framed by the simple *passe-partout* method, show the varied, colorful effects you can create with very little expense, few materials, and no complicated skills.

A piece of picture glass (thinner than ordinary glass), cut by a glazier to the same size as the mat. Non-reflecting glass can be purchased in some places, but this is apt to be expensive. Also, the texture of this glass will blur, slightly, the lines in the picture.

A piece of cardboard for the backing, the same size as the mat and the glass.

Passe-partout tape in your chosen color.

Scissors and a single-edge *razor blade*.

Picture hangers. The kind consisting of a ring and two prongs are especially good, but you can also use the adhesive type.

You will also need *glue*, a *pencil*, a *ruler*, a *soft cloth*, and a *window-cleaning solution*.

Although passe-partout framing doesn't offer such varied effects as you can get with molded frames, you'll be surprised at the possibilities it does offer for bringing out the best in your pictures. When choosing tape and mat paper for a frame, consider the colors in the picture. Notice, for example, how the green mat around the picture of the baby on page 116 complements the red cushion, and the dark blue frame seems to pull everything together. The dark blue mat and bright yellow tape pick up the dominant colors in the child's painting on the same page. Hold your picture against several combinations of mat and tape before choosing your colors.

Technique

1. Place the picture on the mat and adjust it so that the edges of the picture are parallel with the edges of the mat. Use the ruler to check this. Once your picture is in place, put a weight on it and make very small marks at the corners with a pencil.

2. Remove the picture from the mat. Put a thin layer of glue on the back of the picture. Carefully lay the picture on the mat, making sure the corners fit inside your penciled marks.

3. Fasten the picture hangers to the cardboard backing. First, pencil two dots at an equal distance from the top of the cardboard and bend the prongs so that they lie flat along the cardboard. Alternatively, you can stick on adhesive hangers.

4. Clean the glass thoroughly with the cloth and some window-cleaning fluid. This step is most important, as a smudge on the inside of the glass will be impossible to remove once you've applied the tape to the edges. (It is possible to buy special cloths for cleaning and polishing picture glass—useful for mirrors and windows as well.)

5. Now lay the mounted picture over the cardboard and place the glass on top. Cut

Far left: laying the picture (having applied glue to the back) on the mat paper.

Left: covering the mat and picture with a piece of clean glass.

Right: folding the tape over the edge of the mounted picture and glass. Trim the ends of one strip of tape before applying the next.

Below: mitering the corners of the tape. Be very careful to cut only through the tape, without scratching the glass. Miter the corners underneath, as well.

four lengths of tape. Each piece should be about $3\frac{1}{2}$ inches longer than the side it will be attached to.

6. Lay a piece of tape along one edge of the glass, with about half of its width overlapping the glass, and press it down. Gently lifting the edge of the assembled layers, fold the edge of the tape underneath. Trim the ends of the tape so that they are flush with the corner of the glass. Repeat this process on the remaining three sides.

7. Now miter the corners of the tape. Using a razor blade, make a diagonal cut from the inside corner of the tape (on the glass side) to the outer corner. Peel away the bit of tape left from the upper strip, then lift the edge of this strip and remove the excess bit of tape cut from the lower strip. This will remove any bulges from the corners, giving the frame a neat finish. Repeat the mitering on the back of the picture and on the remaining three corners. Give the glass a final polish, and your passe-partout-framed picture is now ready to hang.

Mobiles for Children
17

Everyone loves mobiles. These charming airborne decorations brighten any room. Fish and bird designs are especially popular, possibly because the motion of the mobile in the air suggests swimming or flying. But you can also use different kinds of animals, little people, flowers, or abstract shapes. Construction paper is useful, though if you want stiff shapes, you may prefer poster board. Cellophane makes pretty trimmings for the shapes and catches the light as the mobile moves.

Simple mobiles can be very effective. Practice making some with lightweight, inexpensive materials. Ping-Pong balls can be decorated in a variety of ways. Try making a "Snow White and the Seven Dwarfs" mobile for your child's bedroom or playroom. Paint simple faces on the Ping-Pong balls. Make little wigs of yarn and small felt caps, and glue these on. Pieces of construction paper, rolled into small cones, make the bodies.

One of the prettiest mobiles you can make uses the technique of setting in clear plastic (see pages 57 through 60). Use shallow round molds (such as the petri dishes used in laboratories). Pour a thin layer of plastic into each mold, and lay wild-carrot plumes on top of the partly set plastic, fanning out the leaves in a star pattern. Cover the leaves with another thin layer of plastic. When the disks have hardened, remove them from the molds and drill a small hole near the edge of each disk. Use strong thread to attach the disks to copper or brass mobile wires (see balancing technique on page 124). Hang the mobile where it will catch the sunlight and make lacy patterns on the wall. This mobile would also look pretty in an enclosed porch.

The very simple mobile shown opposite makes a pretty decoration for a child's room and is one that your child can help to make. It requires only a few materials and very little time and effort. You will have to do some of the steps yourself, but your little girl or boy can help with some of the others, such as blowing balloons, cutting the pieces

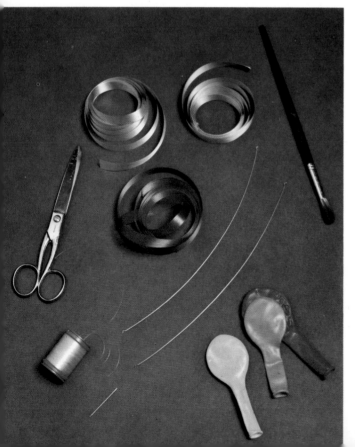

Right: mother and daughter share a happy moment admiring the colorful mobile they have just made together, using a few simple inexpensive materials.

Left: the materials you'll need to make a mobile like the one in the picture. If your craft shop does not stock mobile wires, buy a roll of wire and cut it into suitable lengths yourself with pliers.

of ribbon, and puncturing the balloon.

To make this ribbon-sphere mobile, you'll need these materials:

Balloons: three round ones.

Ribbon, the shiny kind that sticks to itself when moistened, used for wrapping presents. Choose three different colors that go well together. The colors will run when wet, so if you want a streaked, irridescent effect, you can blend two or more colors. Otherwise, make each sphere of a single color.

Wire. Use two pieces of curved wire with hooks on each end. These mobile wires are available in varying sizes in craft shops. Or you can buy wire and cut it yourself. Use a fine grade of steel wire (brass or copper wire is more suitable for heavier mobiles) and cut it with fine-nosed pliers.

Thread. Ordinary sewing thread (white or black as you like) will do. Or you can use monofilament nylon thread, which is virtually transparent.

A brush. A fairly large, soft-bristled kind is best.

Other materials you'll need are: some *scissors,* a drinking *glass,* a *pin,* some *paper clips,* *paper towels,* a *needle,* and some *glue.*

Technique

1. Inflate a balloon to a diameter of about 4 inches (or more or less, depending on the size you want the ribbon spheres to be). Knot the opening securely.

2. Cut 7 lengths of ribbon of one color: First fill the glass with cold water. Take a diameter of the balloon. Make sure that you keep it on the widest part of the balloon. Overlap the ends at least 1 inch. Cut the ribbon. Now, using this first strip as a guide, cut 6 more lengths of ribbon.

3. Wrap the ribbon around the balloon: First fill the glass with cold water. Take a strip of ribbon and wrap it around the balloon, keeping to the widest part. Holding the ribbon gently but firmly in place with one hand, apply water with the brush to the overlapping ends. Add the other strips in the same way, crossing the balloon at regular intervals. Overlap the ends at different points.

4. Again using the brush, moisten all the surfaces of ribbon. Don't oversaturate the

Far left: inflating the balloon. A diameter of 4 or 5 inches makes a good-sized sphere.

Left: cutting strips of ribbon. These should go around the widest part of the balloon, with a 1-inch overlap.

Right: moistening each ribbon where it overlaps. A light touch is required for this part.

Below: after all the strips have been wound around the balloon they are thoroughly moistened. Take care to avoid oversaturating the strips, as this may cause the ribbon to slide a bit on the balloon.

ribbon, but do make sure that it is thoroughly moistened. Set the wet balloon gently on a piece of paper towel.

5. Open a paper clip and poke one end through the edge of the knot. Hook the other end over a clothesline or drawer pull. Make sure that the balloon and ribbon are not touching any surface. Put a piece of paper towel beneath the balloon to catch the drips.

6. Prepare two more ribbon spheres in the same manner. Allow them to dry thoroughly, which will take several hours.

7. When the ribbon has completely dried, pierce the balloon with a pin and remove it. You are now ready to assemble the mobile.

8. Thread a needle and pull the thread through a ribbon so that the knot is on the underside. Leave about a foot or more of thread on the sphere. Repeat for the other two spheres.

9. Tie one end of a thread over one of the mobile wire hooks. Adjust the length to suit yourself. Attach another sphere to the other end of the wire in the same manner. You need not make the second thread the same length as the first—in fact, the mobile will

123

Left: brace yourself!
A pinprick explodes the
balloon, which can now
be removed.

Right: once the ribbon
has dried, it is stiff
enough to hold the
spherical shape.

Right center: a job for
mother—sewing a thread
through the ribbon at
one point. The thread
will be attached to the
mobile wire.

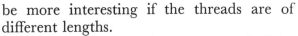

be more interesting if the threads are of different lengths.

10. Attach the third sphere to one end of the second wire.

11. Tie a thread around the middle of the first wire and tie the other end to the other hook of the second wire. Adjust the length so that the spheres will not bump into each other. Tie another thread around the centre of the second wire and loop it temporarily over a lamp fixture or some other high object.

12. Adjust the balance by moving the thread connecting the two wires and the one leading up from the second wire. When the mobile balances, put a dab of glue beside each of the two knots to keep them from slipping along the wire.

13. Attach the top thread to the ceiling or light fixture.

This colorful ornament will delight your child, especially, because she's helped to make it herself.

The individual spheres, by the way, make lovely Christmas tree ornaments. Unless you have a very big tree, you'll want to make them a bit smaller, with a diameter of 3 inches or less. Use smaller widths of ribbon for these. The ribbon can easily be split into any width you prefer. You can also attach a tiny Christmas tree ball inside the sphere, using transparent thread.

Right: the finished mobile—a shiny, colorful object
to decorate the room of the proud little girl who
shared the excitement of making it with her mother.

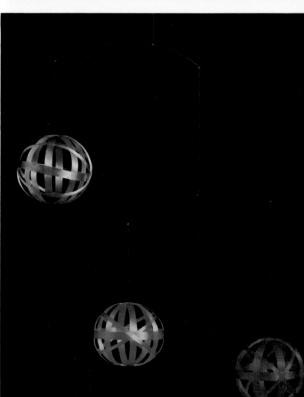

124

More Mobiles

Once you've got the "hang" of mobiles, you can devise all sorts of interesting variations—sophisticated modern mobiles, elegant mobiles, and mobiles for special occasions (see page 127).

The mobile at right uses a piece of poster board about 10 inches square. Using a compass, draw six concentric circles, leaving a little space between them. Leave a 3-inch circle in the center. Cut the circles with a scalpel or scissors. Paint a Ping-Pong ball bright red. With a long needle and a piece of nylon thread, string the ball and the circles together. Make a knot at the point where each circle is to rest, then push the needle through the center of the board. Attach the mobile to the ceiling or fixture.

The fish was drawn on a piece of foil and faced with another piece in a contrasting color. Cut scales and glue them on. Cut segments as shown in the diagram. Make notches in a mobile wire. Attach a segment to each notch with a short piece of thread. Attach a small tree ornament to a shorter wire and balance the fish on the other end.

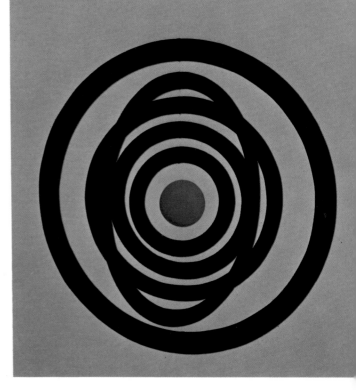

Above: inspired by the Space Age, this clever mobile is fascinating to watch, and easy to make as well. Concentric circles of poster board are cut as shown in the diagram, strung together along with a Ping-Pong ball painted red, and attached to the ceiling or to a light fixture.

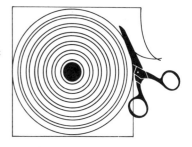

Left: this amusing segmented fish follows the float around through the air. Draw the out-line on stiff green foil (face it for added stiffness) and cut it into four pieces. Foil scales in a different color add interest. The float is simply a bright Christmas decoration.

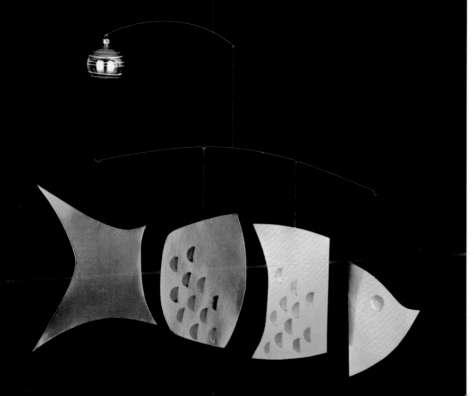

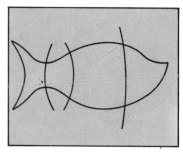

Ideas for Christmas

noel

A Crèche from Paper

A crèche, or Nativity scene, makes a beautiful Christmas decoration that recalls the basic meaning of the season. This paper crèche is both appealing and easy to make. Your family can join in making it from pieces of bright-colored construction paper. Arrange the figures on a table or mantlepiece with some sprigs of greenery.

You can brighten the Yuletide scene in your home with decorations like those on the last two pages. The project to be featured is picked out in the key that heads the page. Full instructions and also diagrams are provided on the next few pages.

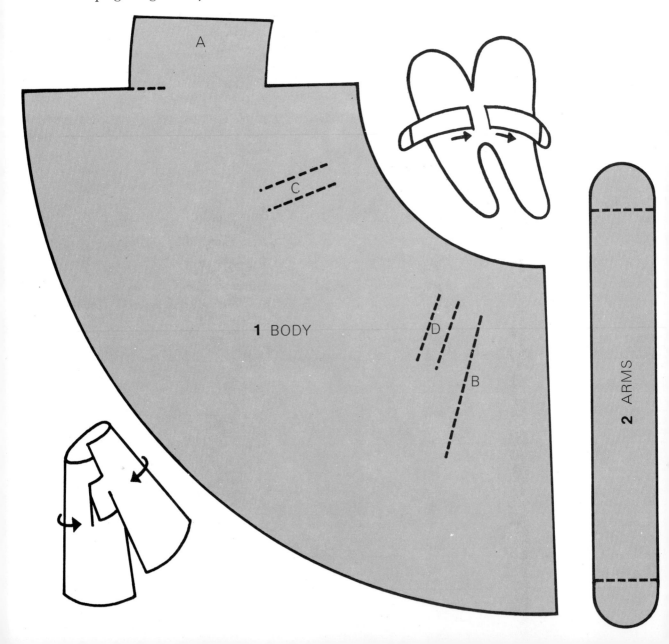

A

C

1 BODY

D

B

2 ARMS

Pattern pieces for the six figures—Angel, Mary, Joseph, Shepherd, King, and Infant—are reproduced actual size on these four pages. The small diagrams illustrate the way the pieces are put together. A minimum of gluing is required, so that you can undo the figures and store them easily.

Materials needed for the crèche include:
Ping-Pong balls (6) for the heads.
Construction paper in several colors, including white, gold, and black.
White paper, including one sheet of light-weight and several sheets of tracing paper.
Scissors, and (optional) a *razor blade.*
A *paintbrush,* and several colors of paint, including black.

Wooden sticks (2). These should be flat, narrow, and very lightweight.

You'll also need a *pencil,* a *ruler,* straight *pins, glue,* and cellophane *tape.*

Plan your colors carefully in advance to help give each figure individuality. You may want to make two more kings and devise different crowns and decorations for them. An additional shepherd or two would then be needed to balance the kings. Vary the colors for these extra figures.

On the next page are detailed instructions for making the Angel. The other figures are constructed in essentially the same way, with some variations, explained in the special instructions given for each figure.

7 DECORATION

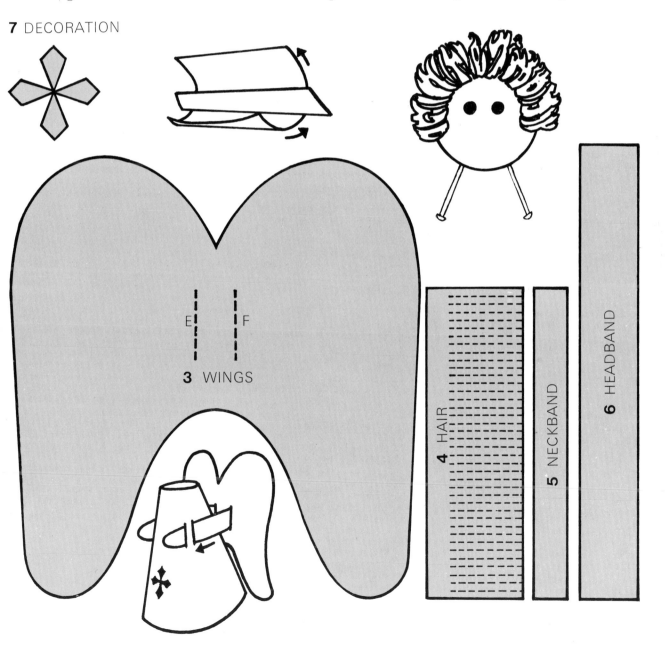

E   F

3 WINGS

4 HAIR

5 NECKBAND

6 HEADBAND

The Angel. Trace pattern pieces (1) through (7) directly from the book. Cut (1) and (2) from the stiff white paper; (3), (5), (6), and (7) from the gold paper; and (4) from the lightweight white paper. Cut slits at marks B, C, D, E, and F, preferably with a razor blade, and cut along the dotted line at Tab A. Curve the arms and body by pulling them under the edge of the ruler several times quickly. Curve the wings lengthwise. Insert Tab A of body through Slot B. Slip the arms through Slots C and D of the body, as shown in the diagram. Glue decoration (7) to front of body. Take one of the Ping-Pong balls and paint two black dots on it for the eyes. Make the "hair" by cutting many slits on (4), as indicated on the pattern, then curling it well with the ruler. Attach this strip to the head with glue as shown in the drawing. Make (5) and (6) into rings by curling them and sticking the ends together with glue. Attach (5) to the head with a small piece of tape. Set (4) on the neck of the body. Insert two straight pins in the head and squeeze them together to insert them into the neck.

Mary. Cut pieces 1, 2, 4, 8, 9, and 11. *Special instructions:* cut *two* pieces of (2), one of stiff white paper, and one of the dress color, cutting this latter piece off at the dotted lines. Glue these two pieces together to make sleeved arms. In cutting (8), trim off at dotted line G, but do *not* cut slots. Trim the cloak slightly to square the corners. Cut (9) out of the same color as (8), and curl both. Glue (9) to form a ring, and attach it to the center back of (8), flaring downward and overlapping (8) slightly. This will make a stand-up collar. Slip arms through body slots and glue to the front of the body as shown in the photograph. Make white hair as for Angel, but divide it into two sections. Attach them to the side of the head. Attach the headdress (curved) to top of head.

Joseph. Cut 1, 2, 4, 5, 9, and 10. *Special instructions:* cut one of (2), in robe color, plus white hands. Cut *entire* cloak and fold straight across top to make a collar. Cut slots I and J, and insert arms first through these and then through body, as in Angel diagram. Use (9) for crown of hat. Remove center of (10), and attach (9) to (10) with

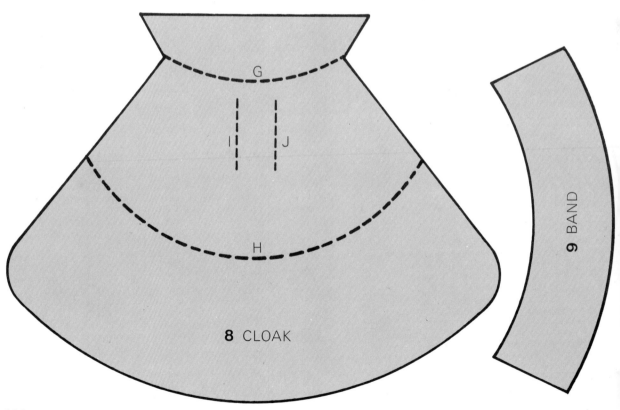

8 CLOAK

9 BAND

bits of tape. Make white hair, and attach it as a beard. Attach hat with tape. Cut a stick to about 6 or 7 inches, paint it with the chosen color, and glue it to left hand.

Shepherd. Cut 1, 2, 4, 8 (between G and H only), 9, and 10. *Special instructions*: make arms as for Joseph. Make the beard from black paper. Curve the hat brim upward. Make a staff and attach it to left hand.

King. Cut 1, 2, 4, 8, 12, 13, and 14. *Special instructions*: make arms as for Joseph. Trace (14) twice, once for circle and once for gold star. Fold collar of cloak as for Joseph, but trim in a curve. Assemble crown by first overlapping edges of (12) and gluing, then gluing (13) into a ring, then taping (12) inside (13). Make a stiff black beard as for Shepherd.

Infant. Cut 4, 15, 16, 17, 18, and 19 (two). *Special instructions*: make arms as for Joseph. Attach decorations to body and glue body together at back. For head, slice off one third of a Ping-Pong ball. Attach a short strip of white hair (made of thin paper), and cover this with (15). Insert pins in head and attach head as for other figures.

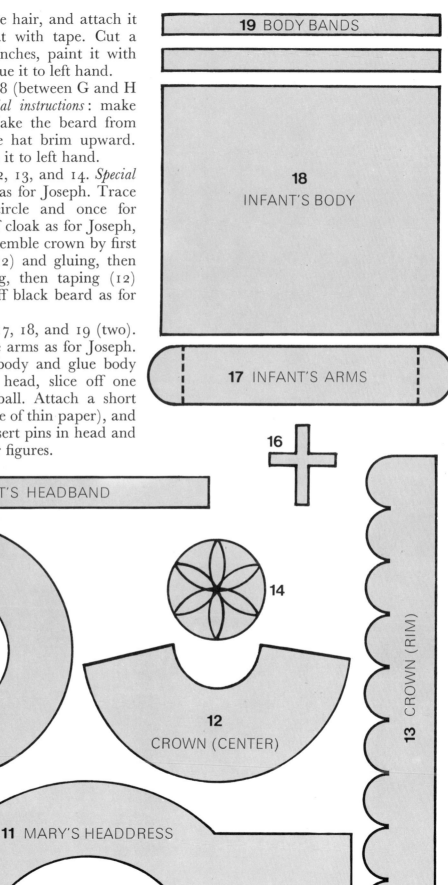

19 BODY BANDS

18 INFANT'S BODY

17 INFANT'S ARMS

16

15 INFANT'S HEADBAND

10 HAT BRIM

14

13 CROWN (RIM)

12 CROWN (CENTER)

11 MARY'S HEADDRESS

Fancy Gift Wrappings

The only trouble with beautifully wrapped packages is that one almost doesn't want to open them. Make these decorations well in advance, so that they can be put under the tree and admired for a few days. And if the recipients use a little care unwrapping the gifts, you can even save the decorations and put them on packages next year!

A charming decoration for a child's gift is a parade of ducks. Using the picture on page 126 as a guide, draw and cut out pattern pieces for the body and head (one piece), the bill, the wing, and the eye (two circles, one smaller than the other). Trace each pattern three times, using a different colored paper each time, so that you have—for example—one yellow wing, one blue wing, and one pink wing. Cut out the pieces and mix them up, so that each duck is made of contrasting colors. Glue a wing and eye onto each duck and then glue the ducks onto the wrapped package. Glue a bill beside each head.

For a very simple, but pretty, decoration, silhouette designs on packages with the "snow" that comes in an aerosol can. Cut out shapes, such as a Christmas tree, a star, or a bell, and lay one of the patterns on the wrapped package. (Use plain, dark colored paper for the wrapping. Colored foil is especially nice.) Spray the "snow" lightly over the top of the package. Remove the pattern. The shape will be clearly outlined against the "snow."

The Fish

This shimmery fish is a real eye-catcher, especially if you make it in colored foil. First wrap the package in plain paper. On a contrasting colored paper, draw the outline of a fish, large enough to cover most of the top of the package. Glue this to the package. Paint an eye on the fish, using a non-water-based paint and making one small dark dot on top of a large white one.

Trace the scalloped pattern above and cut duplicate pieces of foil. Cut along the dotted lines to within $\frac{1}{4}$ of an inch of the straight edge, as indicated on pattern. Curl the scales using a ruler, as shown in the diagram on page 129.

Starting at the tail, glue down the strips (cut to length). Apply a small amount of glue along the straight edge, leaving the cut scales free. Stagger the rows so that each scale overlaps a break between scales in the previous row.

Left: the basic pattern for the fish scales. Cut as many rows of scales as required to cover the body of the fish.

The Rose

To make this pretty rose, you need construction paper in green, yellow, and either pink, white, or red. You also need some tracing paper, a ruler, a pencil, glue, and scissors.

First, trace the five pattern pieces on this page. Then cut five of each piece, using your chosen colors. You should then have 10 leaves and 15 petals. Also, cut a small piece of yellow paper, about 1 inch square, for the stamens, and another 1 inch square of green for the base.

Cover the package to be decorated with plain paper. (See photograph for one possible color scheme, or try dark blue paper with a white rose, or pale green with a red one. Make the folds as invisible as possible.)

Curl all the leaves downward with the edge of a ruler (see diagram on page 129). Curl the petals upward. Apply a dab of glue to the base of each leaf and stick the leaves onto the green base, alternating large and small leaves in a circle.

Stick the petals down in similar fashion, beginning with the largest and finishing with the smallest, overlapping the petals slightly.

Make the stamens. First cut slits along one side (see directions for making Angel's hair on pages 129-130). Curl this fringed edge. Join the edges of the paper to form a small tube (see diagram below) and glue together. Cut four tiny slits in the bottom of the tube, thus making four tabs. Apply glue to these tabs and press the stamens into place in the center of the flower.

Finally, apply glue to the base and stick the flower onto the package.

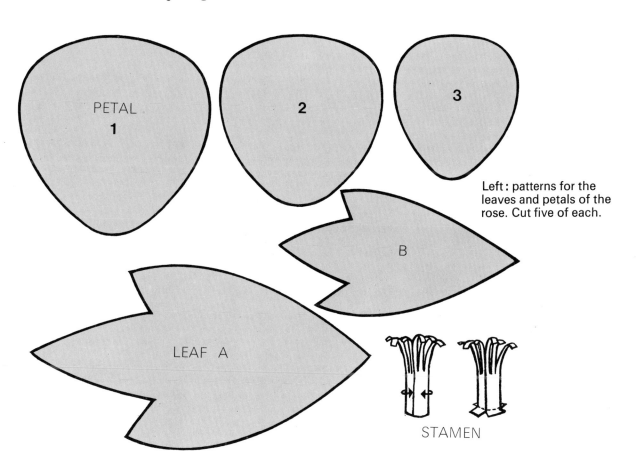

PETAL 1

2

3

Left: patterns for the leaves and petals of the rose. Cut five of each.

B

LEAF A

STAMEN

Foil Decorations

You don't have to be an origami expert to fold this beautiful star and the matching candle decoration. They may look complicated, but once you've started working with the paper, you'll catch on quickly.

Begin with the candleholder, as it uses basically the same folds as the star, but is smaller and simpler. First trace the pattern at right directly from the book, duplicating solid and dotted lines. Cut a strip of foil $4\frac{1}{2}$ by 24 inches. Lay the pattern on the white side of the foil, and—using a pointed instrument, such as an orange-stick—score the paper lightly along all the lines, both dotted and solid.

Keep the pattern before you as a guide to the direction of the folds. Following origami style, we shall call folds that go *up*

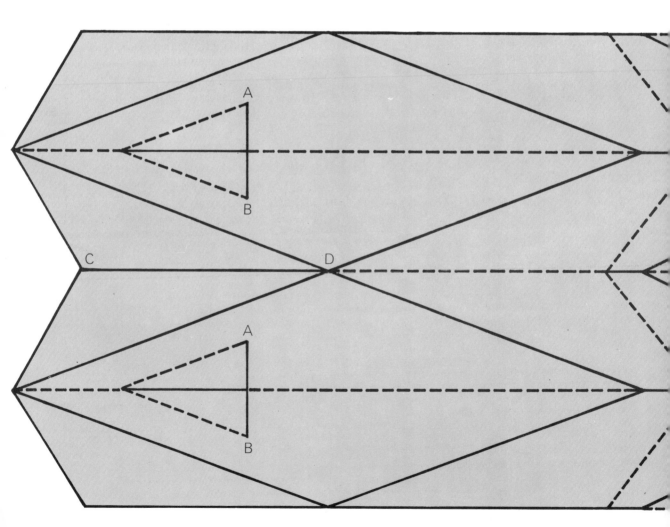

on the foil side "mountains" (the solid lines), and those that go *down* on the foil side "valleys" (the dotted lines).

Begin by accordion-pleating the strip on the straight, crosswise lines. (First, fold each line in *both* directions. This will make the paper more flexible.)

After you have made your accordion pleats, make the other folds. Then stick the ends together with cellophane tape. Insert the candle first in a small ordinary holder to make it steady, and slip the foil decoration around it.

For the star, trace the pattern below. Stick the tracing paper well down into the gutter of the book. You can adjust the drawing later, smoothing out lines where necessary.

You will need a piece of gold or silver foil 50 inches long by 11 inches wide. Duplicate the basic pattern as many times as necessary. Using a razor blade, cut along the base line of the tiny triangles (A-B). Cut also along the center line C-D and repeat these cuts throughout the length of the foil. Using the pattern as a guide for mountains and valleys, make the various folds as for the candle decoration, beginning with the accordion pleats. Fold first in both directions for flexibility.

When you have finished folding, glue the flaps together underneath. Pinch the ends of the strip together, run a needle and thread once through, near the bottom, and tie this in a knot. Open the star and tape the edges together. Attach a loop of string or a hook for hanging the star on the Christmas tree or on a light fixture.

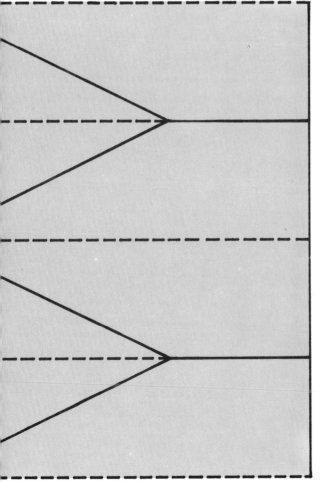

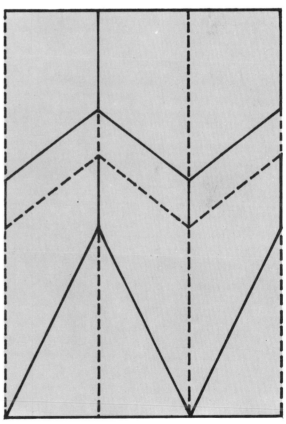

Left: the pattern piece for the star decoration.
Above: the pattern piece for the candleholder.

135

A Christmas Mobile

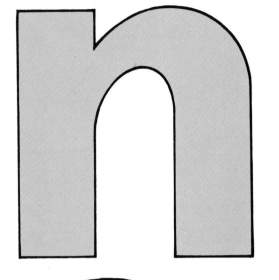

The "Noël" mobile is easy to make (first see the general instructions for making mobiles, on pages 120 through 124). Use construction paper in four colors. Trace the letters on this page, and cut two of each letter. Lay the two halves of each letter so that one is a mirror-image of the other. Apply glue to each half. Lay a piece of black thread lengthwise on one, and then place the other half on top, forming a "sandwich." Attach the four letters to a mobile wire.

Tree Ornaments

You can make some elegant tree ornaments using balls of Styrofoam, ribbon, braid, sequins, and beads. Cut lengths of ribbon to go around the circumference of the ball. With a straight pin, secure each piece of ribbon at top and bottom. Completely cover the ball with ribbon, and add braid (if desired) and other decorations. To avoid giving the ball an elongated shape, start with a few short strips, a little less than half the circumference, so that they do not quite reach the top and bottom. Subsequent whole strips will cover these areas. Also, avoid overlapping the ribbon width wise any more than necessary. Apply a tiny bit of white glue along the edge of one ribbon, just before wrapping the next ribbon around the ball. This way, you can just barely overlap the ribbon with no risk of gaps. Make a loop at the top with a piece of braid, or crochet a tiny loop and insert a wire hook.

For gilded pine cones, first attach a bit of wire at the top, forming a loop. Suspend the cone and paint the tips of the scales gold.

Questions and Answers about Marketing Your Wares

Handmade items are highly prized in our increasingly machine-made world. People enjoy owning something that someone else made with care and attention, using his or her own two hands, and once you become expert at a craft you'll probably discover that there's a demand for your handiwork. What's more, you'll want to go on producing hooked rugs, or mosaics, or whatever, long after your own home and the homes of close friends and relatives have all the rugs or mosaics they need. The next step is obvious: turn your hobby into an enterprise that is not only satisfying, but profitable as well.

Remember, though, that even if you can make a little money selling your handiwork, the important thing is that your work gives you pleasure and a sense of accomplishment. Don't let it become a burden.

With that cautionary note in mind, you may still want to consider the marketing possibilities of your craft. Here are some especially selected questions and answers to shed some light on the subject.

I've been making bead necklaces for ages now, and friends have been saying how beautiful they think they are. Many people have wanted to buy them, and I've let them have necklaces for just a few cents each. I'm getting rid of so many now that it occurs to me that I might put everything on a more commercial footing. What are the chances of success?

The fact that your friends have offered to *buy* your necklaces, rather than just accept them as gifts, is an indication that you may have a saleable product. But so far, you're selling only to friends, and at a price below the cost of your materials and time. The acid test is: will customers—not friends or relatives, but strangers right off the street—pay a reasonable price for your handiwork? If so, there is a good chance that you have the nucleus of a profitable business.

I make candles and intend to sell them locally. I'm finding it difficult to decide how much I should charge for them. Is there a sensible way of going about it, rather than plucking figures out of the air?

Your first task is to figure your cash investment. First, list your materials—such as wax, dye, molds, wicks—plus any other expenses, such as gas or electricity, or running the car (if you must go some distance for your supplies). You will need to do some careful figuring to determine the average cost of materials that go into making a 10-inch taper, for example, or a 4- by 5-inch sandcast candle.

Next, you must put a price on your own labor. This is difficult. Suppose you could earn $3 an hour working as a secretary, and you assume that this is a fair price for your labor. Also assume that you can make a molded candle in two hours. Do you then add $6 to the cost of the materials and charge, say $6.50 for a candle? Not if you want to sell it! Small-scale enterprises—in which the output is low, relative to the time invested—must put a lower cost on labor. When you become more productive, you can put a more realistic price on your labor.

As you can see, figuring a fair price for an item is a tricky business. Your best bet is to prowl the boutiques and department stores and see what they're charging for similar candles. Pay special attention to handmade candles—these will tend to fetch a higher price than mass-produced ones. Of course, as a beginner, you'll be wise to charge a bit less, in order to attract business. Later, when you're better established, you can raise your prices a bit.

What is the best way to get it known that I'm starting a little business selling my macramé work?

Start with the simplest—and in some ways the best—form of advertising: word of mouth. Tell your friends. Ask them to tell *their* friends and simply to spread the word around. If your work is good, people will admire it. Wearable crafts, such as macramè, get around and get noticed.

I've been doing decoupage for a year or so, and selling items occasionally. Now I feel confident enough to broaden out and do things on a larger scale. How can I go about getting my merchandise known in the area?

Supplement your word-of-mouth advertising by having some simple business cards printed up. This can be done for a very small sum of money. They should have your name, address, phone number, and some brief description of what you make. (See the sample card opposite.) Don't be too technical or obscure in your description. Remember that you'll be handing these cards out to people who may be unfamiliar with the craft fields.

For just a bit more money, you can get a whole brochure printed. This does not have to be fancy. In fact, the more homemade it looks (as long as it is still attractive), the better off you will be. If possible, take a few close-up photographs of your work in black and white. Write a simple description of what you do, mentioning any awards you may have won. List some sample prices. Add any catch phrases you think will attract buyers. Type this material and arrange it, along with the pictures, on a folded sheet of paper. (Add more pages, if you like.) Paste everything in place, and take the brochure to a fast-service letter shop.

There are, of course, many different printing processes, and some of them are quite expensive. But the last few years have seen a mushrooming of street-level copying and printing stores. They will photocopy letters for you, or for very modest charges (usually less than $5 per 100 copies) print your brochure. Additional copies beyond the first 100, if ordered at the same time, are considerably cheaper. As with your cards, the brochure should have your name, address, and any other information that a customer might need in order to get in touch with you.

Once you have cards, brochures, products, and a host of loyal friends touting your craftsmanship in every direction, what else

Above: examples of classified ads (top), a business card (center), and a display advertisement (below).

should you do? First of all, exploit all possible avenues of free promotion. For example, many supermarkets, schools, churches, and other organizations have bulletin boards where members or customers can post announcements. This is a good place to put cards and brochures. Don't be bashful about going into any of the shops that you already patronize and asking if you can leave a stack of your brochures or cards on their counter. Chances are they'll agree, so long as your products are not in direct competition with theirs.

The beauty shop you patronize might be willing to let you set up a small display of your decoupage. Women waiting for their appointments will have a chance to inspect your work at leisure and may want to get in touch with you. Make sure that the display includes a neatly lettered card with your name, address, telephone number, and the information that these items, as well as many others, are for sale.

Check to see if any craft shows or exhibitions are going to be held in your area. If so, take a small space and see what kind of reception the public gives you. Don't expect to make a financial killing, but if you're reasonably lucky you will be able to recover the cost of your entrance fee (if there is one) and your transportation. More important, you'll get to talk directly to your customers and find out how they feel about your work.

Make an appointment with a reporter on your local newspaper—the smaller the paper the better for your purposes. Show him your work, explain that you're a local resident, and tell how your hobby gradually became a business. If you're convincing and interesting, the editor may print a story about you and your work. After all, you are local news as much as anyone else, and that is what his publication is all about. If at all possible, ask him to include the information that your work is for sale at a certain address, or get your telephone number worked into the story. Incidentally, unless the cost of producing your objects is very high, it's a good idea to leave a sample of your craft

work with the reporter who interviews you. A sample of your work is a good way of reminding the writer of you and your skill.

If any of the radio stations in your locality have interview or homemaking programs—or, for that matter, any kind of show, even remotely connected with your work—by all means give them a call. You may be invited to come to the station and tell your story on the air. Such an opportunity can be a big plus in getting your business venture moving along more swiftly.

So, you see, your promotion work is cut out for you. There's no way of telling in advance which of these techniques will be most profitable. Try several or all of them and see which brings the best results.

People who watch me making my string sculptures are fascinated, and I seem to spend a great deal of my time teaching them how to do it! Can I capitalize on my "teaching" skills?

Yes, you can. First of all, try your nearest YWCA or YMCA or 4-H Club. These organizations are often looking for teachers of handicrafts and they may well have a place for you.

Also, get in touch with local clubs in your neighborhood. These can be community groups, garden clubs, or fraternal organizations. These groups often have a surprising amount of trouble finding interesting program material for their meetings. Offer to put on a demonstration of how you do your work, so that they can see, step by step, the way you achieve your results. At the close of your demonstration, you can almost always (by prearrangement) give the audience the opportunity to buy your work.

Is it too ambitious to think of advertising my wares in the newspaper? Can you give me any hints on how to write an advertisement that will really attract attention?

Advertising in a paper means spending money, but you needn't spend very much. Consider the classifieds. Most papers have a column or page of classified ads, and these have a high readership. Fortunately, the cost of inserting such an advertisement is often well within the most modest budget.

As for writing the ad, simplicity and clarity should be your guiding principles. Most of the time, you'll have the proverbial 25 words or less to work with. Start off with a word or phrase that should catch the eye, and if possible have it printed in boldface type. Continue with a brief description of the objects. Wind up with your name, phone number, and/or address.

Try different kinds of ads. Don't just write one and stick with it. Experiment to see which approach gets the best results. Try one ad based on price, one based on quality, one based on usefulness. Keep tabs on your results, and when you find that a certain kind of ad brings more sales than others, concentrate on it.

For a bit more money than it costs to run a classified, you can run a small display ad, which will attract more attention. This should follow the general form of your business card (see example on page 139). In addition to the local newspaper, try advertising in small local magazines, college newspapers, church bulletins, and the like.

A friend and I have launched a batik-print operation. I print the fabrics, and she makes up the garments. We've been very successful so far, but on a small scale, in and around our town. The favorable response makes us wonder if we might attract customers in other areas. How should we go about this?
If your work sells well locally, there's a good possibility of expanding into other territory. But this is a big decision to take. Increased demand entails increased production. If you and your friend are already working full-time on your batik, you'll have to hire people to work for you, and you'll find that your work as craftsmen will diminish, while your work as businesswomen—promoting, selling, and planning your production—will increase.

A compromise between remaining small and becoming a big operation is to find an agent to sell your work for you. You may still have to hire (and train) people to help produce the crafts, but you can carry on mainly as a craftsman. Such agents are known as jobbers. The problem is that your present production will probably be too small to interest most jobbers; but you may come upon one who *is* interested.

There's another kind of agent, however, that you might use quite successfully, even if your production is low. Get a little help from your friends. Some of them may work in large companies, or belong to large organizations. They may be willing to act as your salesmen on a commission basis, which means that they get a percentage of the price of every item they sell.

Do large department stores generally show any interest in buying crafts on a small scale?
It's quite possible that these stores—small gift shops and boutiques as well—would be willing to sell your crafts for you. Generally, they will do this on a consignment basis (although some will buy crafts from you outright). This means that you leave an assortment of items with the store and are paid for them only as they sell. For example, you may leave two or three dozen items with the store, stop by a couple of weeks later, receive payment for five or six items that have been sold, and leave some more items to replace these.

To get such an arrangement under way, select some of your most attractive items for a display. Remember that space is at a premium in a store, so you will not be able to spread out your wares in great profusion. Make up a display sign to attract attention, and work out a price schedule on the items. Most stores work on a 50 to 100 per cent markup when they carry material on consignment, so allow for this in your pricing.

Make a list of stores that might be interested in taking your work on consignment, and call upon the store owners (or department buyers, in the case of large stores). Show your samples and explain that you will develop a small display and keep the store supplied with items. If the store agrees to your proposition, work out a schedule for you to call in on a regular basis. When you leave work to be sold, list each item carefully, and have the owner, or buyer, sign a receipt for them. Make sure that the wholesale price (the amount the store is going to pay you) is listed plainly with each item. The next time you go in you should receive payment for the work that has been sold. You can then replace these with new merchandise. Make a note of the items that move most quickly and the ones that seem to be nailed to the shelves. If a certain item fails to sell after a reasonable length of time, take it back and replace it with something else.

Is it against the law to sell my crafts off the front porch? We live in one of the most scenic parts of the state, and the road runs right past our door.
Your first move is to check the zoning regulations in your area. If they allow you to do so, go ahead and open your shop. You may want to make your retail outlet a year-round operation, and devote your basement or a spare room to shopkeeping. Keep regular hours and make sure the store is open at these times so that customers will always know where and when to find you.

Now that I've started to earn a little money with my tie-dyed fabrics, I'm wondering what—if anything—I should do about the tax man.
Several factors are involved here, including the amount of money you earn over a year, and whether or not you already file a tax return (either your own or a joint return with your husband). It's a good idea to check with an accountant as to what you must declare and what you can deduct as business expenses.

In any case, keep a careful record of your income and expenditure. Even if you do no more than break even at first, you may need these figures later, when and if your work becomes a profitable enterprise and comes under the scrutiny of the IRS.

Suppliers

The increasing popularity of handicrafts in recent years has been accompanied by an increase in the number of shops providing materials for the hobbyist and in companies manufacturing these materials. If you live in or near a good-sized town or city, you should have no trouble finding materials for any of the crafts described in this book. A hobby shop, or a large department store, can provide you with anything from rug yarn to plastic resin. Some shops specialize in materials for particular crafts; a lapidary supplier, for example, can equip you with stone-polishing materials and jewelry findings. Consult your Yellow Pages—or the Yellow Pages for the nearest large town—for the names and phone numbers of craft suppliers.

Many mail-order houses provide materials for the craftsman. Look in the advertisement section of one of the hobby magazines for the names and addresses of these suppliers.

Once you get really involved in a particular craft you'll want to investigate the possibility of buying materials in bulk, at a discount. Here again, check the Yellow Pages to see if it lists any wholesale dealers in your materials. Discuss your situation with them. Another approach is to write to the manufacturer of the products you use. You may be able to get a discount on large orders.

For Your Bookshelf

To perfect your skills in any of the crafts introduced in this book, you may want to do some further reading. The books listed here include those we found most helpful. They are listed in the order in which their subjects are introduced in this book.

Making Mosaics
by Edmond Arvois, Sterling Publishing Co., (New York, 1964); Oak Tree Press (London, 1965)

Mosaics
Herder & Herder (New York, 1972); Search Press (London, 1972)

Bead Necklaces
Herder & Herder (New York, 1969); Search Press (London, 1969)

Simple Jewelry
by R.W. Stevens, Watson-Guptill (New York, 1967), Studio Vista (London, 1966)

Painting Bottles and Glasses
Herder & Herder (New York, 1970); Search Press (London, 1969)

Make Your Own Rugs
by Dietrich Kirsch and Jutta Kirsch-Korn, Watson-Guptill (New York, 1971); B.T. Batsford Ltd. (London, 1970)

Techniques of Rya Knotting
by Donald J. Willcox, Van Nostrand Reinhold Co. (New York, 1971)

Rugmaking
by Nell Znamierowski, The Golden Press (New York, 1972); Pan Books Ltd. (London, 1972)

Candle Making
Herder & Herder (New York, 1972); Search Press (London, 1971)

Setting in Clear Plastic
by Katherina Zechlin, Taplinger Publishing Co., Inc. (New York, 1971); Mills & Boon (London, 1971)

Color and Dyeing
by Harriet Tidball, Craft and Hobby (New York)

Tie & Dye Made Easy
by Anne Maile, Taplinger Publishing Co., Inc. (New York, 1971); Mills & Boon Ltd. (London, 1971)

Batik
Herder & Herder (New York, 1969); Search Press (London, 1972)

The Book of Batik
by Ernest Muehling, Taplinger Publishing Co., Inc. (New York, 1967); Mills & Boon Ltd. (London, 1967)

Enamel Without Heat
by Stephen J. Schilt and Donna J. Weir, Sterling Publishing Co., Inc. (New York, 1971); Oak Tree Press Ltd. (London, 1972)

Flower Pressing
by Peter and Susanne Bauzen, Sterling Publishing Co., Inc. (New York, 1972); Oak Tree Press Ltd. (London, 1972)

Dried Flower Book: A Guide to Methods and Arrangements
by N. C. Carico and J. C. Guynn, Doubleday & Co., Inc. (New York, 1962)

The Complete Book of Decoupage
by Frances S. Wing, Pitman Publishing

Corp., (New York, 1965); Sir Isaac Pitman & Sons Ltd. (London, 1968)

Decoupage: A New Look at an Old Craft
by L. Linsley, Doubleday & Co., Inc. (New York, 1972)

Pebble Polishing
by Edward Fletcher, Sterling Publishing Co. (New York, 1973); Blandford Press Ltd. (London, 1972)

Macramé
The Golden Press (New York, 1970); Pan Books Ltd. (London, 1972)

Practical Macramé
by Eugene Andes, Van Nostrand Reinhold Co. (New York, 1971); Studio Vista (London, 1971)

Framing
by Eamon Toscano, The Golden Press (New York, 1971); Pan Books Ltd. (London, 1972)

Picture Framing
by Max Hyder, Pitman Publishing Corp. (New York, 1964); Sir Isaac Pitman & Sons Ltd. (London, 1963)

Make Your Own Mobiles
Sterling Publishing Co., (New York, 1965); Oak Tree Press Ltd. (London, 1966)

How to Make Mobiles
by John Lynch, The Viking Press, (New York, 1953)

The World of Christmas
by Rosemary Lowndes and Claude Kailer, Angus & Robertson (London, 1972)

Make Your Own Party Decorotions
by Ilse Strobl-Wohnschlager, Watson-Guptill (New York, 1970); B.T. Batsford Ltd. (London, 1969)

Tinfoil Decorations for Christmas
Herder & Herder (New York, 1967); Search Press (London, 1967)

Craftwork in Color
Better Homes & Gardens, The Meredith Corp. (New York, 1966); William Collins & Sons Ltd. (London, 1971)

Picture Credits